BRITISH CHEESE COOKERY

'Cheese has always been a food that both sophisticated and simple humans love'
M.F.K Fisher, 'The Art of Eating', 1954

'Everything is better with cheese added'
Steve Parker, 2023

Following a corporate career working for an international brewer and wine distributor, Steve Parker opened an award-winning cheese shop, delicatessen and wine bar in South West London.

He judges in international food and drink competitions, including the British, Artisan, International and World Cheese Awards and has featured in industry publications including *Speciality Food Magazine, Decanter, Off Licence News and Wine Merchant.*

He is now an experienced writer and speaker on his favourite subjects of cheese and wine, with a particular interest and focus on the cheeses and wines of Britain.

His first book *'British Cheese on Toast'* was published by Headline Home (Hachette) in 2020 and his second book *'Cheesespotting'* was published by Toad Cottage Press in 2023. This is his third book.

BRITISH CHEESE COOKERY

Simple and creative recipes using British cheeses

Published by Toad Cottage Press
Copyright © 2024 Steve Parker

First published as Cook British Cheese!
in Great Britain in 2023 by Toad Cottage Press

All rights reserved. No part of this publication may be reproduced, stored in a retrieval system, or transmitted, in any form or by any means without the prior permission of the publisher, nor be circulated in any form of binding or cover other than that in which it is published and without similar condition being imposed on the subsequent purchaser.

A catalogue record for this book is available from the British Library

ISBN:9798342634076

www.steveparkercheeseandwine.com

steve@steveparkercheeseandwine.com

Twitter : @stevecheesewine

Instagram : stevecheesewine

Updated : 01.11.24

To My Harshest Critics and Biggest Fans

Selina, Holly, Felicity

Contents

Introduction to the Recipes 11

The Recipes 15

- Hot Dishes 19

- Cold Dishes..73

- Side Dishes..83

- Sweet Dishes 109

- Snacks and Nibbles................................117

Thank You 141

Recommended Cheese Shops & Restaurants ...145

Index of Cheeses 157

General Index 167

Introduction to the Recipes

My love for cooking with British cheese started when I opened Hampton Cheese and Wine Company in 2010. Prior to this I had always enjoyed spending time in the kitchen creating my own dishes using innovative combinations of foods. I have never been a follower of other people's recipes, preferring to experiment with different ingredients, textures and flavours.

Opening a cheese shop and wine bar presented me with the perfect opportunity to indulge my creativity on my customers, with the added bonus that they paid me for the dishes!

The recipes in this book have been devised by myself, most of which are entirely original but some have been inspired by other dishes and modified to use British ingredients. You will not therefore find recipes for classic cheese based dishes such as mac 'n' cheese, cauliflower cheese or lasagne. As delicious and popular as these dishes are, there are numerous very good recipes for them to be found in other books.

The book and its recipes are intended to focus on interesting and tasty combinations of flavours and not on advanced cooking techniques. There are no recipes for pastries, cakes or anything else requiring more than the bare minimum of cooking. This is a book written for the busy hungry cook.

For each of the cheeses, basic information is given in the following format…
Name of Cheese (1234 Name of Dairy)

1 = Milk Source (C = Cow, G = Goat, S = Sheep, B = Buffalo)
2 = Treatment (P = Pasteurised U = Unpasteurised T = Thermised)
3 = Rennet (V = Vegetarian A = Animal / Traditional)
4 = O = Organic

Treatment

P = *Pasteurised milk is heated to kill all the naturally occurring bacteria and enzymes. Designed to kill any detrimental bacteria but in doing so it kills everything. Usually undertaken when milk from multiple sources is used, as any traceability is impossible. To distinguish it from other processes, pasteurisation involves heating the milk to 72°C for 15 seconds or 63°C for 30 minutes.*

T = *Thermised milk is heated to between 57°C and 68°C for 15 seconds. This kills some, but not all, of the natural bacteria and enzymes in the milk, thereby retaining more of the natural flavours. Thermised milk is technically unpasteurised.*

U = *Unpasteurised milk refers to all milk that is not, by definition, pasteurised.*

U/P = *Available as either unpasteurised or pasteurised.*

Rennet

Rennet is a key part of the cheesemaking process as it is used to coagulate the milk and set the curd into a solid form.

A = *Animal rennet, sometimes referred to as traditional rennet, is an enzyme obtained from the stomach lining of an unweaned veal calf, kid or lamb.*

V = *Vegetarian rennet can be made either by using moulds that produce enzymes that are similar to rennet, or by genetically modifying moulds to produce the rennet enzyme.*

L = *In the case of some cheeses, no rennet is used and instead the curds are set by the action of lactic acid, which is converted from naturally occurring lactose in the milk.*

A/V = *Available as either animal or vegetarian rennet.*

Organic

Where indicated with an 'O', the milk has been produced using organic farming methods. (O) indicates that the cheese is made as an organic version and a non-organic version.

The cheeses are all British and the other ingredients, where possible, are British with substitutions being made for more commonly used foreign versions. British produced rapeseed oil is used instead of olive oil, locally made crème fraiche is widely available instead of the French version but sadly there are no native grown olives, so compromises have been made.

I am a massive supporter of English and Welsh wines and have visited over 150 vineyards in the last year alone. It is not surprising therefore that several of the recipes have used wine as an ingredient, British of course. I would urge you to get out, visit some vineyards and try some of the excellent wines, both still and sparkling, that we are making these days.

Each recipe uses a particular style of cheese and specific cheeses are recommended as being suitable for the recipe. If you are unable to get the recommended cheeses just use whatever you fancy or you are able to source.

For more adventurous cooks the recipes can be used as a guide. Feel free to experiment and free style by swapping the key ingredients for others to see what results you get.

If you create some of the recipes, or your versions of them, please make sure you tell the world about them on social media tagging @stevecheesewine.

The Recipes

Hot Dishes

Cheese and Bacon Bread and Butter Pudding 20

Cheese, Apple and Onion Bread Pudding 22

Roastine..24

Hot Ploughman's on Toast...27

Cheese and Squeak 29

British Beer Fondue 32

Somerset Rarebit 35

Joe Bangles' Burger Wellington 37

Cumberland Toad in the Hole...40

Cheese and Wine Soup 43

Kentish Nut Roast 45

Three Cheese Gnocchi Bake..48

Green Vegetable Pizza 50

Baked Blue Balls 53

Red Red Onions 55

Tartiflette Tatin 57

Welsh Barley Risotto...60

Summer Holiday Sausages 63

Cheese and Wine Chicken 66

British Bloomy Bake 69

Melting Muffins...71

Cold Dishes

Stilton Special Salad 74

Double Mediterranean Style Salad 76

Quick Cheese & Wine Pâté 79

Cheesy Coleslaw 81

Side Dishes

Filled Roasties 84

Chrosti 86

Potato Amanda 88

Anglo Aligot 90

Ulster Blue Potato Cake 92

Ginny's Y^3 Yorkshire Yorkshire Yorkshires 94

Giant Yummy Beans 97

Lincolnshire Roasted Sprouts 99

Northampton Beer Cobblers 101

Blue Goat Mushrooms 104

Goat's Cheese Nuggets 106

Sweet Dishes

Wensleydale, Ginger and Rhubarb Crumble 110

Lancashire Fruit Cake Parcels 112

Blue Cheese and Chocolate Hobnobs 114

Snacks & Nibbles

Sheep, Pear, Honey 118

Goat, Mango, Marmalade 120

Blue Breadcakes 122

West Country Dip 125

Double Gloucester Bakes..127

Single Gloucester Crisps..129

Yeasty Cheesy Puffs..131

Spicy Cheese Scrunchies...133

Cheshire Flapjack...135

Frozen Blue Cheese Dust..137

Rocks and Honey...139

Hot Dishes

Cheese and Bacon Bread and Butter Pudding

Possibly the ultimate in comfort food, this recipe combines so many favourite things into one simple to prepare and delicious dish. It can be served as a breakfast, lunch or supper dish - it works equally well at any time of day.

Ingredients

Serves 4 people

- 20g unsalted butter
- 1 shallot - finely chopped
- 4 rashers streaky bacon (smoked or unsmoked as preferred)
- 4 eggs
- 100g British crème fraiche
- 150g hard full flavoured cheese (see options below)
- 4 slices granary bread - one side thickly buttered - cut into halves
- 40g butter for buttering the bread and and the ovenproof dish

Method

- Melt 20g of butter in a small saucepan and add the chopped shallot allowing it to soften and gently cook, but do not let it brown.
- Remove from the heat and allow to cool.
- Cut the bacon into thin strips across the rasher and place the strips into a pre-heated non-stick frying pan. Cook them until lightly browned stirring to stop them becoming crispy. Remove from the heat and place to one side.

- Crack the eggs into a large bowl and whisk well.
- Add the crème fraiche to the eggs and mix well before adding the shallots.
- Add 100g of the grated cheese and mix well into the egg mixture.
- Lay the slices of buttered bread into a buttered ovenproof dish and pour the cheesy eggy mixture all over ensuring that all of the bread is soaked.
- Sprinkle the cooked bacon over the top of the soaked bread then sprinkle the remaining 50g of grated cheese over the top of everything.
- Place the dish into an oven at 200°C/180°C Fan/Gas Mark 6 for about 20 - 30 minutes until a medium brown and the pudding has set firmly (check with a small knife inserted into the pudding)

Recommended Cheeses

There are a number of suitable cheeses as long as they can be easily grated. In recipe trials, the following worked particularly well…
Wiltshire Loaf (CPV Brinkworth), Birdoswald (CPVO Slack House), Norfolk Dapple Vintage (CUV Ferndale), Anster (CUA St Andrews)

Options

- The recipe can be easily converted to a vegetarian version by substituting sliced mushrooms for the bacon.

Cheese, Apple and Onion Bread Pudding

Bread Pudding is not to be confused with Bread and Butter Pudding as in the previous recipe. Instead of cooking the buttered bread in a cheesy cream to give a lighter dish, in this recipe the bread is soaked and cooked more like a cake, with a denser texture. Any bread can be used for this recipe but the secret is to let it get stale for a few days before using. Cheddar is the perfect cheese for pairing with cider, apples and onions.

Ingredients

Serves 6 people

- 650g stale sliced bread - about 14 thick slices with crusts on
- 350ml cider
- 1 tablespoon dried sage
- 1 onion - finely diced
- 1 Granny Smith apple - skin on - finely diced
- 2 teaspoons English mustard
- 200g Cheddar - grated
- 25g unsalted butter

Method

- Tear the slices of stale bread into a large mixing bowl and pour the cider over allowing it to all soak in and become soggy for about 20 minutes.

- Add the dried sage, diced onion, diced apple and mustard and mix well.
- Add the grated cheddar and mix well using clean hands.
- Use the butter to grease the inside of a shallow cake tin.
- Spoon the mixture into the cake tin and press down into the corners and smooth the surface.
- Place the dish into an oven at 200°C/180°C Fan/Gas Mark 6 for about 30 minutes until a medium brown and the pudding has set firmly (check with a small knife inserted into the pudding).

Recommended Cheeses

There are a large number of excellent cheddars made in Britain so a selection representing different regions have been recommended…
Plaw Hatch (CUVO Plaw Hatch), Wiggold (CPVO Abbey Home Farm), Lion Hotel 1868 (CPV Blaenafon Cheddar), Briddlesford (CPV Briddlesford Farm)

Options
- If preferred, pear can be used instead of apple, giving a slightly sweeter flavour or pear and apple mixed.

Roastine

Based upon the iconic Canadian dish from Quebec, *'Poutine'*, this British version uses roast potatoes instead of chips and an English red wine gravy.

The crisp potatoes, rich gravy and stretchy cheese make this a perfect comfort food, served by itself straight from the oven or as a filling side dish.

Ingredients

Serves 2 people as a main course or 4 as a side dish

- 50g unsalted butter
- 2 long shallots - finely diced
- 1 clove of garlic - crushed or grated
- 75ml full-bodied English red wine (options below)
- 35g plain flour
- 400ml beef stock
- 1 tablespoon Worcestershire sauce
- 500g potatoes - peeled and cut into 4 cm chunks
- 40ml rapeseed oil
- 150g Raclette style cheese - thinly sliced (options below)

Method

- Melt the butter in a medium saucepan, add the shallots and cook for 3 minutes, stirring occasionally, until clear but not browned.

- Add the garlic and stir for 1 minute, add the wine and stir, scraping any sticky bits from the pan until it reduces to a sticky paste.
- Stir in the flour and keep cooking until a thick paste has formed before adding the stock and Worcestershire sauce whisking until it is smooth.
- Stir and simmer while stirring from time to time until the gravy has reduced to the desired thickness, ideally coating the back of a spoon.
- Place the potatoes into a saucepan of cold water, bring to the boil and allow them to boil for 3 minutes. Drain immediately and return to the saucepan, place the lid on and holding it on tightly shake the pan twice, lightly roughing up the surface of the potatoes.
- While the potatoes are being brought to the boil, heat the oil in a roasting pan in an oven at 200°C/180°C Fan/Gas Mark 6.
- Remove the pan from the oven, tip in the potatoes and using a spoon, ensure they are all coated in the oil before placing back into the oven.
- Turn the potatoes every 15 minutes and just as they start to brown, use a potato masher or the back of a large spoon to lightly crush the potatoes before finishing the in the oven until they are a crunchy light brown.
- Lay the slices of cheese over the potatoes and let them melt for a few minutes before pouring the gravy over the top and serve.

Recommended Cheeses

The key to this recipe is a cheese that melts easily such as…

Westcombe Curd (CUA Westcombe), Mrs Kirkham's Curd (CUA Mrs Kirkham's), Batch Farm Curds (CUV Batch Farm), Yester Fior di Latte (CPV Yester Farm)

Recommended Wines

The gravy requires one of the more robust English red wines such as…

Trevibban Mill Black Ram Red, Ark Ripasso Noir, Burn Valley Rondo, Barnsole Pinot Précoce

Options

- Leave the skin on the potatoes for extra texture and nutrition.
- For a vegetarian version use vegetable stock instead of beef and yeast extract instead of Worcestershire sauce.

Hot Ploughman's on Toast

This recipe was inspired by one that I created for my first book 'British Cheese on Toast'. As with so many traditional recipes handed down through the generations, there are many different interpretations of what constitutes the original. What is beyond doubt is that it should contain cheese, bread and pickles, so these form the basis for this recipe, with a number of other well matched ingredients.

Ingredients

Makes one cheese on toast

- 1 slice crusty white bloomer or granary bread depending on preference
- 1 tablespoon Branston Original Pickle (other brands are available)
- 1 slice of your favourite traditional cooked ham
- ½ Granny Smith apple - cored and thinly sliced
- 75g of your favourite Cheddar - grated
- 2 pickled onions - drained and thinly sliced
- 1 tablespoon British crème fraiche

Method

- Toast the bread lightly on both sides then spread the pickle evenly on one side of the toast.
- Lay the ham on top of the pickle and then arrange the sliced apple over the top.

- Mix the grated Cheddar, sliced onions and crème fraiche to a rough paste and spread over the top of the apples, ensuring that it reaches right to the edges of the toast.
- Place into the oven at 200°C/180°C Fan/Gas Mark 6 on a baking tray for 3-4 minutes to warm through then place under a pre-heated hot grill until the cheesy top is bubbling and starting to brown.

Recommended Cheeses

Traditionally a ploughman's would always be made with cheddar, but in recent years other cheese styles have been substituted, but for the purposes of this recipe, choose your favourite cheddar. Although there are many cheddars made in Britain, I would always recommend traditionally hand-made versions including…

Westcombe (CUA Westcombe Dairy), Hafod (CUPAO Holden Farm Dairy), Isle of Mull (CUA Isle of Mull), Dale End (CUVO Botton Creamery)

Options

- Pickled onions can be swapped for spring onions if you prefer it less 'bitey'.
- Sliced pear can be used in place of the apple for a sweeter flavour.

Cheese and Squeak

Bubble and Squeak is a traditional British dish made by using up the left overs from a Sunday roast and has existed since at least the 18th century. This variation uses the same principles but instead of the traditional mashed potato is more rustic and textured by using crushed potatoes. The addition of spring onions and a strong flavoured cheese gives it an extra bite and tanginess.

Ingredients

Serves 4 people

- 4 rashers of unsmoked streaky bacon - cut into thin strips across the rasher
- 500g small potatoes with skin on or chunks of peeled larger potatoes
- 100g cooked greens (cabbage, sprouts, kale, etc)
- 4 spring onions - cleaned and chopped into small rings
- 150g strong flavoured cheese - grated
- 25g unsalted butter
- 25ml rapeseed oil

Method

- Place the bacon strips into a large pre-heated non-stick frying pan and cook them until lightly browned stirring to stop them becoming crispy. Remove from the heat and place to one side.

- Cook the potatoes in a large pan of boiling water until just tender (a sharp knife just pierces them) then remove and allow to steam dry.
- Place the cooked potatoes into a large bowl and roughly crush (not mash) them, adding the cooked greens, spring onions, cooked bacon strips and half of the grated cheese.
- Mix roughly to maintain the coarse texture.
- Heat the oil and butter in the same frying pan then add the potato mixture and using a spatula or large spoon press it into the pan forming a thick cake.
- Continue cooking over a low heat, occasionally turning the mixture over so that the caramelised base gets mixed through and further parts of it become golden and crispy, each time pressing it down into the pan again.
- When there are sufficient crunchy golden parts for your personal taste, sprinkle the remaining half of the grated cheese over the top and place under a pre-heated hot grill until the cheese melts and bubbles.
- Slide the finished cake out onto a board and cut into slices as required.

Recommended Cheeses

There are a large number of cheeses that can be used in this recipe with the only condition being that it is full flavoured and easily grated. Recommended cheese are…

Balcombe Breeze (CPV Balcombe), Fat Cow (CPV Highland Fine Cheese), Holbrook (GUA St James Cheese), Wandering Ewe (SUA Wandering Ewe)

Options

- The recipe can be easily converted to a vegetarian version by substituting sliced mushrooms for the bacon.

British Beer Fondue

Traditional fondue is made in Alpine regions using locally made mountain style cheeses and local wines. In this adapted British version, the cheeses are made in the Alpine style and the wine is replaced with beer. If this is the first time you have made a fondue, it will seem like an enormous amount of cheese, but be assured, it will all melt into the beer and result in a rich creamy warming dish.

Ingredients

Serves 2 people

- 400g cheese - grated
- 25g cornflour
- I clove garlic - peeled
- 200ml beer
- 1 tablespoon lemon juice

Method

- Place all the grated cheese in a bowl and sprinkle with 20g of the cornflour, mixing well to ensure all the cheese is coated.
- Mix the remaining 5g of cornflour with a splash of the beer to make a paste and put to one side for possible use later.
- Take a fondue pan or a heavy saucepan and rub the garlic clove all around the inside. Add the beer and the garlic to the pan and bring the heat up to a low simmer. Remove the clove of garlic and discard.

- Add a small amount of the cheese (half a handful) to the beer and stir constantly. When the cheese has melted into the beer, add a slightly bigger amount and continue stirring.
- Repeat, adding slightly more cheese each time. Do not rush this stage as adding too much cheese too quickly will cause the cheese to form a solid ball, so ensure each amount has melted before adding the next. Do not allow the fondue to boil at any time as this will cause it to split.
- When all the cheese has been added and the fondue is thick and creamy, add the lemon juice and stir.
- Serve from the cooking pan, keeping it warm over a flame or on a hot plate.
- Dip cubes of bread, cauliflower florets, carrot batons or cooked baby potatoes into the fondue.
- If the fondue splits or the cheese starts to form a lump at any time, add the reserved cornflour beer paste and stir in to the fondue using a whisk until it regains its creamy consistency.

Recommended Cheeses

The best style of cheese for this recipe is an Alpine style…
Summerfield Alpine (CUVO Botton Creamery), Haytor (CPV Curworthy), Regatta (CPV Marlow Cheese Co), Ramps Hill (CPV Brinkworth Dairy)

Recommended Beers

A number of styles of beer can be used as long as they are full of flavour without overwhelming the cheese. These have proved to be successful …

Windsor & Eton Knight of the Garter, St Peter's Golden Ale, Innes & Gunn Caribbean Rum Cask, Hiver Amber Beer (adds a hint of honey to the fondue)

Options

- Cider can be used as a replacement for the beer, giving a fruitier flavour to the fondue.

Somerset Rarebit

In my first book 'British Cheese on Toast', there was a whole chapter on *'rarebit'* in its various forms. Even historical recipe books give different recipes and it is clear that there is no one recipe, so this one has been created as a tribute to the cheesemakers and cider-makers of Somerset.

Ingredients

Makes 2 large slices

- 1 teaspoon plain flour
- 1 teaspoon dried sage
- 75ml Somerset cider
- 150g Somerset Cheddar - grated
- 1 teaspoon of Worcestershire Sauce
- 1 teaspoon English mustard
- 2 slices bread - toasted

Method

- Sprinkle the flour and dried sage over the grated cheese, mixing well to coat as much as possible.
- Heat the cider in a medium saucepan to simmering then slowly add the grated cheese, stirring continuously, until it has all been added and a thick creamy paste has formed.
- Add the Worcestershire Sauce and English mustard and stir well.

- Remove from the heat and allow to cool before spreading thickly on hot toast and placing under a pre-heated grill until browned and bubbling.

Recommended Cheeses
Being named after Somerset, it is clear that the only logical option is to use a Somerset Cheddar, either an artisan farmhouse version or a more commercially produced version…

Montgomery's (CUA Montgomery Cheese), Batch Farm (CPAV Batch Farm), Cheddar Gorge (CUV Cheddar Gorge), Wookey Hole (CPV Ford Farm)

Recommended Ciders
Being a Somerset based recipe, it obviously has to be a traditional cider from the county…

Wilding Ditcheat Hill, Pilton Star Ship, Little Pomona Orchard Yarlington Mill, Burrow Hill Sparkling

Options
- An alcohol free version can be made using apple juice instead of cider.
- A different version can be made using beer instead of cider.

Joe Bangles' Burger Wellington

This recipe is dedicated to a gentleman with the social media name of Joe Bangles who promotes cheese by asking famous people what is their favourite cheese. As a tribute, I asked what his favourite cheeses are and used them in the recipe and named it after him. You can of course make your own puff pastry if you choose, but why not use the ready-made version, it's easier!

Ingredients

Serves 4 people

- 2 shallots
- 400g beef mince
- 1 large egg - beaten
- 1 teaspoon rapeseed oil (for oiling surface)
- 1 sheet ready made puff pastry 350mm x 230mm (350g)
- 100g Pitchfork Cheddar - grated
- 100g Stichelton - crumbled
- 100g Ashcombe - sliced

Method

- Finely chop the shallots and place in a bowl with the mince.
- Mix half the beaten egg in the bowl with the shallots and mince.
- Tip the mixture out of the bowl and onto a very lightly oiled surface.

- Using hands mould the mixture into a rectangle about 20cm x 10cm.
- Lay the grated Pitchfork Cheddar along the centre of the mixture and then roll it into a large sausage shape with the cheese enclosed in the middle.
- Lay the sheet of puff pastry onto a floured surface and sprinkle the crumbled Stichelton on the centre of the pastry.
- Lay the Cheddar filled meat mixture on top of the Stichelton and flatten slightly, then lay the slices of Ashcombe on top of the meat.
- Use some of the remaining beaten egg to moisten the exposed edges of the pastry roll it around the meat and cheese log forming a giant sausage roll.
- Carefully turn the wellington over and place onto a buttered baking tray.
- Use any remaining beaten egg to glaze the pastry.
- Cook in the preheated oven at 200°C/180°C Fan/Gas Mark 6 for 30 - 40 minutes until the pastry has browned.
- Allow it to cool for a few minutes before cutting into thick slices.

Recommended Cheeses

These are the cheeses that were chosen by Joe Bangles...

Pitchfork Cheddar (CUAO Trethowan Brothers),

Stichelton (CUA Stichelton Dairy), Ashcombe (CPAO King Stone Dairy)

Options

- If you like the recipe but want to try other cheeses than those chosen by Joe, use a Cheddar, an Alpine style cheese and a blue of your choice.

Cumberland Toad in the Hole

This recipe is a variation on a British classic with the addition of cheese to the batter, along with its best friends sage and onion. It could be made with pretty much any sausage and any cheese but personal experimentation has led me to this combination from Cumbria. The Cumberland sausage is distinctively shaped as a long coiled spiral but can also be bought as a regular sausage shape. It is traditionally flavoured with spices, especially white and black pepper.

Ingredients

Serves 4 people

- 100g plain flour
- 1 teaspoon dried sage
- 1 large egg - beaten
- 150ml semi-skimmed milk
- 100g cheese - grated
- 50ml water
- 8 Cumberland sausages
- 1 medium red onion

Method

- Mix the flour, sage, beaten egg and 100ml of the milk and mix until smooth in a large bowl.
- Add the rest of the milk and beat well with a hand or electric whisk until you have a smooth batter..

- Add the grated cheese to the batter, stir well, cover and leave to rest for half an hour.
- *NB : It is important to leave the batter to rest for at least 30 minutes and anything up to 4 hours.*
- If the batter is too thick after adding the cheese, add the water, a little at a time until it is thick enough to slowly run off the back of a spoon.
- Cut each sausage into four and place in an ovenproof roasting dish.
- Slice the onion into rings and arrange the rings around the sausage pieces.
- Place the sausages and onions into an oven preheated to 200°C/ 180°C Fan/Gas Mark 6 for 10 minutes until just starting to brown.
- Stir the rested batter again and pour over the part cooked sausages.
- Return to the oven and cook for 30-40 minutes until the batter has risen and is a crispy golden-brown colour.

Recommended Cheeses

There are several farmhouse artisan cheesemakers in the Cumbria and their cheeses have the flavour and melting qualities to make this dish perfectly…

Cumberland Farmhouse (CUA Thornby Moor), Trusmadoor (CPVO Torpenhow), Wash Stone (CUA Whin Yeats), Eden Chieftain (CPV Appleby Creamery)

Options

◆ This recipe has been created using Cumbrian products, but could be adapted using a different sausage and cheeses according to personal taste.

Sussex Cheese and Wine Soup

The ancient county of Sussex is well known for making quality cheeses and wines. The chalk of the South Downs and the clay, sandstone and greensand of the Weald lend themselves to perfect conditions for growing grape vines and for grazing dairy cattle. It is therefore an inevitability that the two products are combined in this warming robust soup.

Ingredients

Serves 4 people

- 20g unsalted butter
- 20ml rapeseed oil
- 1 onion - finely diced
- 500g potatoes - peeled and cut into 2cm cubes
- 100ml Sussex still white wine
- 750ml chicken stock
- 200g Sussex firm cheese - grated
- 4 spring onions - cut into fine discs

Method

- Heat the butter and oil in a saucepan and lightly cook the diced onion until softened but not browned.
- Add the cubed potato and cook for 5 minutes stirring to avoid them sticking to the pan.

- Add the wine and stir to deglaze the pan removing any bits that have stuck to the pan.
- Add the stock and bring to the boil then lower to a gentle simmer with a lid on for 20 minutes.
- Add the grated cheese and stir until melted and cook for 5 minutes on a low heat.
- Serve with chopped spring onions scattered over the top.

Recommended Cheeses
The best style of cheese for this recipe is a firm cheese which can be grated…
Olde Sussex (CUV Traditional Cheese Dairy), Idle Hour (CPV Alsop & Walker), Charlton (CPVO Goodwood Home Farm), Ashdown Forester (CPVO High Weald Dairy)

Recommended Wines
Although well-known for sparkling wines, Sussex also produces some top quality still wines…
Bluebell Vineyard Ashdown Chasselas, Stopham Estate Pinot Blanc, Blackboys Vineyard Tickerage Chardonnay, Nutbourne Hedgerow

Options
- Although this recipe uses cheese and wine from Sussex, similar styles from other counties can be substituted.

Kentish Nut Roast

Although many of the recipes in this book are vegetarian, the nut roast is possibly the ultimate non-meat alternative to a traditional Sunday roast.

The reason for naming this as *'Kentish'* is that in the course of my research I met one of the leading nut growers and nut experts in Britain in Kent. Alexander Hunt grows and sells walnuts, hazelnuts and Kentish cobnuts at Potash Farm and is one of the most engaging fascinating people I've ever met and therefore decided to dedicate the recipe to the county in honour of him.

This recipe is enhanced with umami flavour of mushrooms plus the tang of flavour from a thick layer of either vegetarian or traditional rennet cheese through the centre.

Ingredients

Serves 4 people

- 30g salted butter
- 100g brown rice
- 1 onion - finely chopped
- 1 carrot - grated
- 2 cloves garlic - crushed
- 2 tablespoons tomato purée
- 100g chestnut mushrooms - chopped
- 100g any mixed nuts (walnuts, cobnuts, hazelnuts, almonds, cashews, etc)

- 100g fresh breadcrumbs
- 1 large egg - beaten
- 1 tablespoon dried sage
- 1 teaspoon salt / black pepper
- 150g cheese - grated

Method

- Use 10g of the butter to grease a loaf tin.
- Cook the rice according to the packet instructions, drain and cool.
- Melt 20g butter in a frying pan, add the chopped onion, grated carrot and garlic and cook gently for 5 minutes over a low heat.
- Add the tomato purée and mushrooms, stir and cook for another 5 minutes.
- When cool, tip the onion, carrot, mushroom mix into a bowl with the rice.
- Coarsely chop the nuts and add to the bowl.
- Add the breadcrumbs, nuts, egg, sage, salt and pepper and mix.
- Spoon half the mixture into the buttered loaf tin and press down.
- Spread the grated cheese on top of the mixture in the loaf tin then spoon the remaining loaf mixture on top of the cheese, pressing it all down well.
- Cover the loaf tin in foil and cook in an oven preheated to 200°C/180°C Fan/Gas Mark 6 for 30 minutes, then remove the foil and cook for a further 30 minutes until brown and firm to the touch.

Recommended Cheeses

All of the recommended cheeses are made in Kent...

Ashmore Farmhouse (CUV Cheesemakers of Canterbury), Tam's Tipple (CUV Hinxden), Winterdale Shaw (CUA Winterdale), Ottinge Bramshill (CUA Ottinge)

Options

- Although this recipe uses Kentish cheese, other styles can be substituted.

Three Cheese Gnocchi Bake

These small cushions of dough are the base for many dishes in Italian cuisine. Many books will tell you how easy they are to make but nothing is as easy as using a pack of fresh gnocchi - chilled or in vacuum packed pouches. It is also easier to use frozen spinach. The combination of three different cheeses produces a huge range of flavours in this simple, easy to make recipe.

Ingredients

Serves 2 people

- 20g unsalted butter
- 500g fresh chilled or vacuum packed gnocchi
- 300ml British crème fraiche
- 50g soft blue cheese - crumbled
- 50g hard sheep cheese - grated
- 50g Fior di Latte (cow's Mozzarella) - torn into small pieces
- 75g frozen spinach
- 25g walnut pieces - chopped
- 75g fresh breadcrumbs

Method

- Butter a shallow baking dish approximately 30cm x 20cm.
- Empty the gnocchi into the buttered dish and spread it out evenly.
- Heat the crème fraiche in a saucepan until it is lightly simmering.
- In the meantime, cook the frozen spinach according to the packet

instructions - either in a small pan or microwave. When cooked, let it cool.
- Slowly add each of the cheeses to the warm crème fraiche, stirring to incorporate each one into a thick creamy sauce.
- Stir in the cooled spinach and chopped walnuts mixing them in well.
- Pour the sauce over the gnocchi and stir carefully so it coats the gnocchi.
- Sprinkle the breadcrumbs over the top and place in an oven preheated to 200°C/180°C Fan/Gas Mark 6 for about 30 minutes until golden brown and crunchy to the touch.

Recommended Cheeses (choose one from each style)

Soft Blue : *Teesdale Blue (CPV Teesdale Cheesemakers), Yorkshire Blue (CPV Shepherd's Purse), Bledington Blue (CPVO Daylesford), Blue Murder (CPV Highland Fine Cheeses*

Hard Sheep : *Fosse Way Fleece (SPV Somerset Cheese), St Benedict (SUV Lacey's), Redesdale (SPV Northumberland Cheese), Ramsey (SUV Cheesemakers of Canterbury)*

Fior di Latte : *La Latteria (CPA La Latteria), Brue Valley (CPV Brue Valley), Leno (CPVO Hand Stretched Cheese), Velocheese (CPAO Velocheese)*

Options
- Fresh gnocchi is also available as spinach or pumpkin flavours which can add a further dimension if used.

Green Vegetable Pizza

There is no doubt that pizza is one the world's most popular foods and is made with an almost infinite number of ingredients and flavour combinations from the simple to the fully loaded. This recipe is designed to be vegetarian by loading it up with charred green vegetables and a mixture of different cheeses.

Ingredients

Serves 1 or 2 people (depending on how hungry)

- 100g ricotta
- 2 tablespoons ready made green pesto
- Ready made pizza base 20 - 25 cm diameter
- 200g in total of mixed green vegetables - choose from the following… spring onions, mange-tout, courgette strips, tenderstem broccoli
- 25ml rapeseed oil
- 1 teaspoon fennel seeds
- ½ teaspoon celery salt
- 100g Buffalo Mozzarella - torn into strips
- 50g hard cheese - grated

Method

- Mix the Ricotta and pesto together in a bowl and spread the mix over the pizza base, covering to the edges.

- Place the assorted green vegetables into a bowl and pour the rapeseed oil over them then use hands to liberally coat the vegetables in the oil.
- Sprinkle the fennel seeds and celery salt over the vegetables and mix well.
- Heat a griddle pan or heavy based frying pan until very hot then add the vegetables and let them char lightly whilst turning them for about 3- 5 minutes, charring them to your preference. This will allow them to partly caramelise whilst maintaining their crispness.
- Arrange the charred vegetables over the ricotta covered pizza base.
- Arrange the strips of mozzarella across the vegetables covering as much as possible, then sprinkle the grated hard cheese all over the top.
- Place on a pre-heated baking tray in an oven at 200°C/180°C Fan/ Gas Mark 6 for about 20 minutes until it is golden and slightly crispy.

Recommended Cheeses (choose one from each style)
Ricotta : *High Weald (SPVO High Weald Dairy), Kedar (CPV Kedar), Kappacasein (CUAO Kappacasein), Long Lane Ricotta (SPV Long Lane Dairy)*

Mozzarella : *Buffalicious (BUV West Country Water Buffalo) Scottish Buffalo (BPV The Buffalo Farm), Mount's Bay (BPV The Buffalo Dairy), Calveley Mill Mozzarella (CPV Calveley Mill)*

Hard : *Tirkeeran (CPA Dart Mountain Cheese), Harefield (CUV Smart's), Chiltern Cloud (SPVO Marlow Cheese), The English Pecorino (STV White Lake)*

Options

- Fior di Latte (cow's milk mozzarella) can be used as a substitute for buffalo.

Baked Blue Balls

What can be more British than sausages? Now add creamy, tangy blue cheese and walnuts to the sausage meat and it becomes a thing of wonder. Although the recipe has a festive feel, it can be enjoyed at any time of year, either as a supper dish by itself or as a side accompaniment.

Ingredients
Serves 4 people
- 400g pork sausages
- 150g freshly made breadcrumbs (3 - 4 slices using blade in food processor)
- 50g walnut pieces - chopped to the size of peas
- 150g blue cheese - crumbled
- 1 teaspoon dried sage
- 1 egg - beaten
- 1 teaspoon rapeseed oil (for coating hands)

Method
- Slit the sausage skins and squeeze the meat into a large bowl.
- Add the breadcrumbs, the chopped walnuts, crumbled blue cheese, dried sage and the beaten egg and mix well.
- Using hands coated in a very light film of oil, make balls of the sausage mix slightly larger than a golf ball.
- Arrange the balls on a sheet of baking parchment on a baking tray.

- Place in an oven at 200°C/180°C Fan/Gas Mark 6 for about 30 minutes until they are golden and crispy.

Recommended Cheeses

Although any blue cheese of your choice can be used for this recipe, it works best with a medium tangy cheese, not too mild and not too strong…

Northamptonshire Blue (CUV Hamm Tun), Lanark Blue (SUV Errington Cheese), Brighton Blue (CPV High Weald), Dorset Blue Vinny (CPV Woodbridge Farm)

Options

- For an added festive flavour, add 50g dried cranberries to the mixture before shaping into balls.

Red Red Onions

Cheese, onion and sage are the best of friends when it comes to food partnerships and this recipe celebrates this tasty trinity with a distinctive red theme running through it.

Ingredients

Makes 8 halves of filled onion

- 4 large red onions
- 30g unsalted butter
- 50g fresh breadcrumbs
- 2 teaspoons dried sage
- Pinch of ground black pepper
- 100g Red Leicester - grated

Method

- Boil the onions in their skins for 10 minutes, remove and cool.
- Cut each onion in half lengthwise through the root and remove the onion skins leaving the root intact to hold the layers together.
- Scoop out the centre of the onion halves leaving the outer two layers as a shell.
- Finely chop the onion centres and lightly cook them in the butter.
- When they have just started colouring, add the breadcrumbs and stir.
- Remove from the heat and add the sage and a pinch of ground black pepper stirring until all the butter is absorbed.

- Add the grated cheese and mix well.
- Spoon the mixture into the onion shells until they are full and piled up.
- Place the filled onion shells onto a baking tray.
- Cook in an oven preheated to 200°C/180°C Fan/Gas Mark 6 for about 30 minutes until the filling has turned light brown.

Recommended Cheeses

The name of the recipe makes it clear that a red cheese is required and there is nothing more iconic than a Red Leicester, either a traditional version or a more modern take…

Sparkenhoe (CUA Leicestershire Handmade), Devonshire Red (CPV Quicke's), Lincolnshire Red (CUV Lincolnshire Poacher), Red Fox (CPV Belton Farm)

Options

- The recipe calls for Red Leicester, but another red coloured cheese such as Double Gloucester or a Coloured Cheshire would work equally well.

Tartiflette Tatin

Tartiflette is a warming and filling aprés-ski dish traditionally served in Alpine resorts and is made with potatoes, onions, lardons and Reblochon cheese.

This recipe has take the principle of this dish and adapted it with British ingredients and used it to mark a tarte tatin style dish but replacing the fruit with the components of a Tartiflette.

Ingredients

Serves 4 people

- 4 medium potatoes - peeled and sliced 5mm thick
- 25g unsalted butter
- 1 medium onion - peeled and thinly sliced
- 1 clove of garlic - peel and crushed
- 4 rashers unsmoked streaky bacon cut into thin strips across the rashers
- 6 baby gherkins (cornichons) - sliced into small discs
- 150ml soured cream
- 250g washed rind cheese - cut into thin strips
- 1 sheet ready made puff pastry 350mm x 230mm (350g)

Method

- Add the potato slices to a pan of boiling water for 5 minutes to slightly soften them then drain and cool.

- Melt the butter in a 25cm diameter non-stick frying pan and cook the sliced onion over a low heat, stirring occasionally, for about 15 - 20 minutes until the onions start to caramelise without turning too dark.
- Add the crushed garlic and the strips of bacon and stir into the onions allowing them to cook a little before adding the cooled potato slices.
- Add the gherkin slices and soured cream stirring carefully to mix.
- Lay the strips of cheese over the top of everything in the pan and place into an oven preheated to 200°C/180°C Fan/Gas Mark 6 Fan for 3 minutes allowing the cheese to melt completely.
- Remove from the oven and lay the sheet of puff pastry over the top of the pan pricking a few small holes in the pastry to allow steam to escape.
- Using a spoon, very carefully tuck the edges of the pastry into the sides of the pan pushing it under the contents.
- Return to the oven for 30 minutes until the pastry has risen and browned.
- Remove from the oven and run a knife around the edge of the pan to release the pastry from the sides.
- Using oven gloves or a cloth place a plate over the pastry and hold it in place whilst carefully and quickly turning the pan and plate over.
- The tatin should release from the pan and be ready to slice and eat.

Recommended Cheese

The roots of this recipe are Alpine regions with Reblochon being traditionally used, so the recommendations are for cheeses based on that style…

Winslade (CPA Hampshire Cheeses), Stinking Bishop (CPV Charles Martell), St Sunday (CPV St James), Rollright (CPAO King Stone Dairy)

Options

- The traditional use of a washed rind cheese can be changed to an easy melting Alpine style cheese (see page 75 *'Chrosti'* recipe for other Alpine cheeses).

Welsh Barley Risotto

This recipe is based on the principles of a traditional Italian risotto but with a distinctly Welsh twist with the cheeses all being from Wales, the use of a Welsh white wine and the use of leek instead of onion. Using pearl barley in place of rice makes it quicker and easier as well as keep the *'Britishness'*.

Ingredients

Serves 4 people

- 50g unsalted butter
- 2 medium leeks - washed, trimmed and cut into 5mm slices
- 200g pearl barley
- 100ml Welsh white wine
- 750 ml chicken stock - may need a little less
- 75g each of three different Welsh cheese styles

Method

- Remove any rinds from the cheeses and crumble or grate them into a bowl.
- Melt the butter in a large saucepan, add the chopped leek and cook gently over a low heat, stirring until it has softened but not coloured.
- Add the pearl barley and stir to ensure that it is coated in melted butter then cook, stirring for 5 minutes.

- Add the wine and cook, stirring, until the volume of liquid has halved.
- Add the stock about 100ml at a time and stir well each time. Keep a close eye on the pan during this stage as it must not be allowed to dry out.
- Keep adding the stock until it has all been used up and the pearl barley is tender and the risotto still quite runny. This may take more or less stock than the stated quantity, if it needs more it is fine to use water.
- Add the three cheeses, stirring until they have all melted through the risotto and then continue to cook, stirring, for another 5 minutes.

Recommended Cheeses (choose one from each style)

Caerphilly : *Caerfai Caerffili (CUVO Caerfai Farm), Teifi Caerphilly (CUAO Teifi), Caws Chwaral (SUA Cosyn Cymru), Thelma's Traditional Caerphilly (CPVO Caws Cenarth)*

Firm/Hard Cheese : *Caws Dyfi (SPA Aberdyfi Cheese), Hollywell (SPV Monmouth Shepherd), Olwyn Fawr (SUA Cosyn Cymru), Black Bomber (CPV Snowdonia)*

Blue : *Perl Las (CPVO Caws Cenarth), Abaty Glas (CUVO Caws Penhelyg), Blue Wenalt (CPV Brooke's Wye Valley), Mon Las (CPV Caws Rhyd y Delyn)*

Wines that can be used in this recipe

Ancre Hill Chardonnay, White Castle Gwin Gwyn,
Montgomery Seyval Solaris, Llanerch Cariad Poplar White

Options

- For a vegetarian option use vegetable stock instead of chicken.

Summer Holiday Sausages

These vegetarian sausages are packed full of flavours reminiscent of holidays in warmer climates.

Ingredients

Makes 6 sausages

- 300g fresh breadcrumbs
- 2 teaspoons dried basil
- ½ teaspoon black pepper
- 1 red onion - finely diced
- 10 black olives - finely chopped
- 75g sundried tomatoes - finely chopped
- 1 tablespoon capers - finely chopped
- 1 preserved lemon - finely chopped (optional)
- 150g Feta-style cheese
- 2 eggs
- 1 teaspoon rapeseed oil (for use on hands)
- 50g plain flour

Method

- In a large bowl mix together 200g of breadcrumbs, basil, pepper, diced onion, chopped olives, tomatoes and capers and lemon (if using).
- Drain the brine from the cheese and crumble it into the bowl, mixing well.

- Separate the white and yolk of one egg (put the white to one side) and beat the yolk plus the second egg and add to the bowl mixing to form a dough.
- Using your hands, divide the mix into six balls and roll each one into a fat sausage shape (rubbing oil onto hands makes this job much easier).
- Place the flour and 100g of fresh breadcrumbs onto two separate plates.
- Whisk the egg white until it becomes a light foam.
- Roll the sausages lightly in the flour, then coat in the beaten egg white, then roll in the breadcrumbs.
- Place the sausages on to a sheet baking parchment on a baking tray and place in the fridge for an hour to chill and firm up. They can be made up to this point up to a day in advance and kept in the fridge.
- Place the sausages on the baking parchment into an oven preheated to 200°C/180°C Fan/Gas Mark 6 for 30 - 40 minutes until lightly golden brown, turning to ensure even colouring.

Recommended Cheeses

It is important factor that it is a Feta style which has been aged in brine…

Mrs Bell's Salad Cheese (SPV Shepherd's Purse), Fetish (STV White Lake), Medita (SPV High Weald), Ffetys (GPV Y Cwt Caws)

Options
- If preferred, these can be made as a ball rather than a sausage shape and served in a tomato sauce with pasta for a tasty filling supper dish.

Cheese and Wine Chicken

A succulent chicken breast poached in wine, coated in cheese, roasted then served in a wine sauce - it makes the mouth water even writing it.

This recipe is best made using a wine made from Chardonnay but can be made using either a still or a sparkling Blanc de Blancs version. The latter will give a lighter more delicate sauce, whereas the still version gives a silky richness - your choice.

Ingredients

Serves 4 people

- 35g salted butter
- 4 plump skinless boneless chicken breasts
- 200ml chardonnay - sparkling or still
- 1 shallot - finely diced
- 150g chestnut mushrooms - thinly sliced
- Pinch of black pepper - freshly ground is best
- ½ teaspoon dried thyme or 1 teaspoon fresh thyme
- 200g British crème fraiche
- 200g rich soft white rinded cheese - cut into thin strips

Method

- Use 10g of butter to lightly butter a shallow baking dish big enough to hold the chicken breasts.
- Place the chicken breasts into the dish and add 50ml of the wine.

- Place into an oven preheated to 200°C/180°C Fan/Gas Mark 6 and cook for 20 minutes.
- While the chicken is cooking, melt the remaining 25g butter in a saucepan and cook the diced shallot for about 5 minutes until soft but not brown.
- Add the mushrooms and cook them lightly, not letting them colour.
- Add the black pepper and thyme then add the remaining wine and simmer until the wine has reduced to half the volume.
- Add the crème fraiche and stir until smooth then simmer for 5 minutes while finishing the chicken.
- Remove the chicken from the oven and lay the cheese on top of the chicken breasts and place back into the oven for 5 minutes.
- Place a chicken breast on each plate, making sure to serve the reduced wine and any cheese that has melted into it.
- Pour the mushroom and wine sauce over the chicken and serve.

Recommended Cheeses
Baron Bigod (CPA Fen Farm), Bix (CPAO Nettlebed Creamery, Waterloo (CTV Village Maid), Bath Soft (CPAO Bath Soft)

Recommended Wines
Still : *Oastbrook Chardonnay, Chapel Down Kits Coty Chardonnay, Oxney Chardonnay, Balfour Springfield Chardonnay*
Sparkling : *Harrow & Hope Blanc de Blancs, Ridgeview Blanc de Blancs, Hundred Hills Blanc de Blancs, Exton Park RB45 Blanc de Blancs*

Options

- Soft goat's cheese or sheep's cheese provides a tangier flavour when used instead of the cow's cheese in this recipe.

British Bloomy Bake

This recipe is inspired by a combination of a traditional potato gratin and the pub favourite, baked camembert. It is so named because the rinds of these cheeses are described as being 'bloomy'.

Ingredients

Serves 4 people as a side dish

- 750g potatoes
- 250g soft white cheese
- 60g unsalted butter
- 2 long shallots - finely diced
- 2 cloves of garlic - crushed
- 250ml British crème fraiche
- 1 teaspoon dried thyme

Method

- Bring a large pan of water to the boil.
- Peel and slice the potatoes 5mm thick then add them to the boiling water for 5 minutes to slightly soften them then drain and cool.
- Cut the cheese into thin sliced wedges by cutting from the centre.
- Using 10g of the butter, grease an ovenproof dish about 20cm round or square.
- Layer and overlap the sliced potato to resemble fish scales interspersing with the cheese slices so that they are evenly distributed.

- Melt half of the remaining butter (25g) and cook the diced shallot over a low heat stirring for about 5 minutes to soften but not brown, before adding the garlic and cooking for a further 2 minutes.
- Pour in the crème fraiche, add the dried thyme and bring to a simmer letting it stay simmering for 5 minutes to become thicker.
- Pour the crème fraiche all over the potatoes and cheese then place in an oven at 200°C/180°C Fan/Gas Mark 6 for 40 - 50 minutes until it is crisp and golden.

Recommended Cheeses

There are a number of British examples of the style of cheese needed for this recipe. They are usually made as 250g cheeses, meaning that the quantity is exactly right. Amongst suitable options are…
Tunworth (CPA Hampshire Cheese), Gert Lush (CPVO Feltham's Farm) Sussex Camembert (CPV Alsop & Walker), Cornish Camembert (CPV Cornish Cheese),

Options

- A soft creamy blue could be used instead of the soft white cheese for an extra tanginess.

Melting Muffins

These savoury muffins are best eaten while still warm to really savour the tangy cheesy melting centre.

Ingredients

Makes 12 muffins

- 20g unsalted butter
- 180g plain flour - sifted
- 10g baking powder
- ½ teaspoon salt and ground black pepper
- 1 tablespoon dried sage
- 250g cheese - grated
- 1 teaspoon lemon juice
- 2 tablespoons rapeseed oil
- 2 large eggs
- 125ml milk

Method

- Use the butter to grease 12 cups in a muffin tin.
- In a large bowl, combine the flour, baking powder, salt, pepper, sage and half the cheese.
- Mix the lemon juice, rapeseed oil, eggs and milk in another bowl.
- Add the wet ingredients to the flour mixture and stir until just mixed.
- Half fill each muffin cup with the batter mixture.

- Sprinkle 75g of cheddar on top of the batter mixture already in the muffin tin holes.
- Use the remainder of the batter mixture to fill the muffin tin holes.
- Sprinkle 50g of cheddar on top of the finished muffins.
- Bake in an oven preheated to 200°C/180°C Fan/Gas Mark 6 for 20 - 30 minutes until they have risen and are golden brown.
- Remove the cooked muffins from the tin and leave to cool on a wire rack.
- Serve hot or cold.

Recommended Cheeses

The cheese used in this recipe needs to be firm enough to hold it's shape when making the muffins, able to melt easily and have a full flavour. There are many possibilities with the some less common ones being recommended…

Keen's Cheddar (CUA Keen's), Morn Dew (CPV White Lake), Ayrshire Dunlop (CPV Dunlop Dairy), Six Spires (CUV Somerset Cheese)

Options

- For an extra tangy bite, substitute a blue cheese in this recipe.

Cold Dishes

Stilton Special Salad

Stilton with walnuts is a truly classic British pairing combination. Add some juicy pear to lift it a little more, then add bacon to achieve a delicious flavour and texture combination in a fresh green salad. NB - using locally made real honey supports local beekeepers and also gives a better result than commercially produced sugar adulterated honey.

Ingredients

Serves 4 people
- 1 little gem lettuce
- 90g rocket leaves
- 90g watercress
- 4 rashers streaky bacon (smoked or unsmoked as preferred)
- 200g Stilton
- 100g walnut pieces
- 2 pears
- 2 tablespoons cider vinegar
- 2 tablespoons cold-pressed rapeseed oil
- 2 teaspoons wholegrain mustard
- 2 teaspoons honey

Method
- Wash all of the salad leaves and cut across the little gem forming ribbons before mixing all three salads in a large bowl.

- Cut the bacon into thin strips across the rasher and place the strips into a pre-heated non-stick frying pan. Cook them until lightly browned stirring to stop them becoming crispy. Remove from the heat and allow to cool.
- Crumble the Stilton into the salad bowl.
- Add the walnut pieces to the bowl, chopping any pieces that are too large.
- Mix the cooled bacon strips into the salad.
- Wash, core and slice the pears and toss them into the salad (to avoid them turning brown, only do this when you are preparing the salad to eat).
- Whisk the cider vinegar, rapeseed oil, mustard and honey together to make the dressing and toss through the salad immediately before serving.

Recommended Cheeses

There are only five dairies (one of whom is closing) who are legally allowed to make Stilton due to the strict PDO regulations, so this recipe would work with whichever is your personal favourite…
Colston Bassett (CPAV Colston Bassett), Cropwell Bishop (CPAV Cropwell Bishop), Hartington (CPV Hartington Creamery), Long Clawson (CPV Long Clawson)

Options

- The name of the recipe states Stilton but it could equally well be British Blue using your favourite blue cheese.

Double Mediterranean Style Salad

The name of this salad is due to it containing two cheese styles, both with Mediterranean origins. Feta and Halloumi styles are made by several dairies in Britain. This recipe combines the two cheeses in the same dish, using a Greek salad as an inspiration but with quite a few tasty tweaks.

Ingredients

Serves 4 people

- 1 romaine lettuce
- 1 teaspoon sea salt
- ½ cucumber - peeled, halved, seeds removed and cut into 1cm chunks
- 6 tomatoes - cut into quarters
- 1 red onion - thinly sliced
- 18 pitted black olives - halved
- 400g can chick peas - drained and rinsed
- 20 pistachio nut kernels
- 200g Feta-style cheese - drained and cut into 1cm cubes
- 1 tablespoon cold-pressed rapeseed oil
- 1 teaspoon dried oregano
- 250g Halloumi-style cheese - cut into 1cm slices
- 20 fresh mint leaves

Method

- Shred the romaine into 2 cm wide strips, wash and place into a large bowl.
- Sprinkle the salt over the chopped cucumber and tomatoes, leave for 10 minutes then add to the shredded romaine along with the sliced onion.
- Add the halved olives, drained chick peas and pistachios to the bowl.
- Drizzle the rapeseed oil and sprinkle oregano over the Feta-style cheese in another bowl and stir to coat before adding to the salad bowl.
- Finish the salad by tossing everything together before arranging on plates.
- In the meantime pre-heat a dry non-stick frying pan and add the slices of Halloumi-style cheese, cooking each side for a few minutes until they have turned brown, then arrange the cooked slices on the salad.
- Roughly tear the mint leaves and scatter over the salad.

Recommended Cheeses

Feta-style : *Austen (SPV Book & Bucket), Demeter (GUA Wildcroft), Wighton (CPV Mrs Temple's)*

Halloumi-style : *Somerset Goat (GTV White Lake), Sizzler (CUVO Plaw Hatch), Yorkshire Squeaky (CPV Yorkshire Dama), Bermondsey Frier (CUAO Kappacasein)*

- *Options*
- The salad can be further enhanced by adding toasted seeds of your choice (sunflower, pumpkin, sesame) to add crunch and texture.
- Green olives can be used instead of black olives if preferred.

Quick Cheese and Wine Pâté

This simple recipe does not involve any cooking at all and can be completed in only 5 minutes. The tangy saltiness of the blue cheese pairs with the sweet wine to create a beautifully balanced flavour. Delicious served on hot buttered toast or spread on a tender steak and allowed to melt over the meat.

Ingredients
Serves 4 people
- 25g unsalted butter
- 150g soft blue cheese
- 150g soft cream cheese
- 50ml sweet white wine

Method
- Remove the butter from the fridge and allow to soften.
- Using a spoon, mix everything together in a bowl to form a smooth paste.

Recommended Cheeses
The key to this recipe is to choose a blue cheese that is soft and creamy in texture and a few examples are …
Burt's Blue (CPV Burt's Cheese), Blue Clouds (CPV Balcombe Dairy), Beauvale (CPA Cropwell Bishop), Devon Blue (CPV Ticklemore Cheese)

Recommended Wines

This recipe needs a sweet wine and although there are not that many made in Britain, those that are made are excellent including…
Burn Valley Solar, New Hall Purlai Gold, Babu's Vineyard Late Harvest Solaris, Denbies Noble Harvest

Options

- For an alcohol free version, use a mixture of 25ml honey and 25ml apple juice instead of the wine.
- Alternatively leave out the wine and add 50g more soft cream cheese.

Cheesy Coleslaw

This is a flexible recipe designed to made according to personal preference. The base for the slaw is the same, but depending on the style of cheese chosen the flavour will change. Firm cheeses have been recommended but feel free to experiment with your personal favourites or new discoveries.

NB - using locally made real honey supports local beekeepers and also gives a better result than commercially produced sugar adulterated honey.

Ingredients

Makes one large bowl

- 200g white cabbage
- 200g red cabbage
- 1 red onion
- 2 carrots
- 1 Granny Smith apple
- 1 stick celery
- 100g firm cheese - grated
- 100ml British crème fraiche
- 2 tablespoons cider vinegar
- 100ml cold-pressed rapeseed oil
- 2 teaspoons wholegrain mustard
- 2 teaspoons honey

Method

- Finely slice the two cabbages and place into a large bowl.
- Peel and finely slice the red onion and add to the cabbages.
- Peel the carrots and the apple, cut them into 3mm diameter strips and add to the bowl and mix.
- Cut the celery into 3mm strips and add to the bowl.
- Add the grated cheese and mix well.
- Stir the crème fraiche into the bowl mixing well.
- Mix the cider vinegar, rapeseed oil, mustard and honey together in a separate bowl then add to the salad and toss everything together.

Recommended Cheeses

A number of cheeses and styles could easily be used in this recipe but a range of less common firm cheeses have been recommended… Double Devonshire (CPV Quicke's), Volesdale (CUV Coachyard Creamery), Sussex Charmer (CPV Bookham Harrison), Bruton Beauty (CPVO Godminster)

Options

- Although the recipes uses firm cheeses, this has worked equally well with crumbled blue cheese, goat's cheese or even soft curd cheese.

Side Dishes

Filled Roasties

The roast potato is universally loved by many and can accompany numerous dishes, not just roast dinners. This adaptation adds a whole new dimension whilst retaining the very essence of a roastie. Crispy and crunchy outside with a soft yielding pillowy centre, but with full flavoured umami cheese adding a whole new taste to the potato.

Ingredients

Makes 6 potatoes

- 6 oval shaped potatoes at least 5cm in diameter
- 120g semisoft pungent cheese
- 30ml rapeseed oil
- 30g unsalted butter

Method

- Wash and scrub the potatoes leaving the skins on.
- Using an apple corer, remove a core from right through each potato.
- Cut the last 1cm from each end of the cores reserving them for use later.
- Cut the cheese into 6 equal sized pieces of about 20g each.
- Using fingers, press each piece of cheese into the core hole in each potato.
- Plug each potato using two of the ends of the removed cores to block the holes, with the cheese trapped inside the potato.

- Place the potatoes in a roasting pan with the rapeseed oil and butter.
- Roast the potatoes for 45 minutes in an oven preheated to 200°C/180°C Fan/Gas Mark 6, turning and basting them with the oil until crisp and golden brown with a soft centre when tested with a sharp knife.

Recommended Cheeses

The key to this recipe is to use a full flavoured cheese that is soft enough to be pushed into the potato and a semisoft washed rind cheese is ideal for this purpose. There are many good examples of this style of cheese made in Britain and the following are recommended…

Weywood (CTV Cheese on the Wey), Golden Cenarth (CPVO Caws Cenarth), Minger (CPV Highland Fine Cheeses), Highmoor (CPAO Nettlebed Creamery)

Options

- If a less pungent cheese is preferred, then use a semisoft cheese such as…

  Doris (CPV Teesdale Cheesemakers), Dirty Vicar (CUV Norbury Park Farm)

Chrosti

This is a recipe with a made up word as its name; in fact it is a *portmanteau* word made from a combination of *cheese* and *rosti*. A classic dish of a fried cake of shredded potato, sometimes called a *kugel* has been flavour boosted by adding cheese to the recipe, resulting in a super tasty side dish that can be served alongside pretty much any main course.

Ingredients

Serves 4 people

- 500g potatoes
- Pinch of salt
- Pinch of black pepper
- 1 onion
- 4 rashers streaky bacon (smoked or unsmoked as preferred)
- 100g cheese - grated
- 50g plain flour
- 25ml rapeseed oil
- 25g unsalted butter

Method

- Peel, grate and rinse the potatoes.
- Drain the potatoes as much as possible in a colander then completely dry them using a tea towel.
- Season the potato with salt and pepper.

- Peel and grate the onion and add to the grated potato mixing well.
- Cut the bacon into thin strips across the rasher and place the strips into a pre-heated non-stick frying pan. Cook them until lightly browned stirring to stop them becoming crispy.
- Remove from the heat and allow to cool before adding them to the potato and onion mixture.
- Add the grated cheese to the mixture and mix well.
- Using a cooking ring or a mug, mould the mixture into discs about 6cm across and 1.5cm thick, pressing them to ensure they stick together.
- Handling them carefully, dust the discs with flour and place into the fridge for at least 30 minutes to chill and firm up.
- Bring the rapeseed oil and butter to a medium heat in a frying pan.
- Carefully using a slice, lower each disc into the hot pan and let then cook for about 5 minutes until crisp and golden before turning over to cook for a further 5 minutes.

Recommended Cheeses

The ideal cheese for this recipe is an easy melting Alpine style…
Wells Alpine (CPV Mrs Temple's), Llain (CPVO Caws Cenarth), Valley Drover (SUA Hancocks Meadow Farm), Federia (CUA Larkton Hall)

Options

- A soft yolk fried egg served on top of a *chrosti* is truly delicious.

Potato Amanda

Based upon the classic French recipe *Pommes Anna*, but modified by the addition of cheese, shallot and sage. Named for my wife Amanda as a tribute to what she has put up with whilst I have been writing this book and testing the recipes.

Ingredients

Makes 6 Potatoes Amanda

- 60g unsalted butter
- 400g medium-sized potatoes - peeled
- 2 shallots - thinly sliced
- 50g Alpine style cheese - grated
- 1 tablespoon dried sage

Method

- Use 10g of the butter to grease 8 cups in a large muffin tin.
- Thinly slice the potatoes, using the slicer in a food processor or a mandolin.
- Rinse the potato slices in water and dry with a tea towel or kitchen paper.
- Gently melt the remaining 50g butter in a small saucepan.
- Lay some of the potato slices, overlapping in the base of the muffin tin cups.
- Brush a small amount of the melted butter over the potatoes.

- Lay a small amount of the sliced shallot, grated cheddar and dried sage on top of the potatoes.
- Repeat the layers of potato slices, butter, shallot, cheddar and sage.
- Repeat until the muffin tin cups are full, finishing with potato and butter.
- Place a flat baking tray on top of the filled muffin tray and place a heavy weight on top to squash the potato down into the cups for 30 minutes.
- Remove the top baking tray and cook in the oven at 200°C/180°C Fan/Gas Mark 6 for about 40 minutes until tender and golden brown. Test when they are cooked by inserting a sharp knife to test they are soft all the way through.

Recommended Cheeses

As this recipe is named for Amanda, it is only reasonable to use her favourite Alpine style of cheese, but British of course…

Rachael Reserva (GTV White Lake), Mayfield (CPV Alsop & Walker), London Raclette (CUAO Kappacasein), Ogleshield (CUA Montgomery's Cheeses)

Options

- An extra mature Cheddar could be used instead of the Alpine cheese.

Anglo Aligot

This recipe is based upon a French classic, *Aligot,* the stretchy, smooth garlicky potato dish from the Auvergne, typically made with Tomme cheese. The secret to this dish is to use a starchy potato and overwork it to release the starches.

Ingredients

Serves 4 people

- 750g starchy potatoes - Desirée, King Edward or Yukon Gold
- 1 tablespoon sea salt or rock salt
- 2 cloves of garlic - peeled
- 100g unsalted butter - diced
- 250ml British crème fraîche
- 250g Tomme style cheese - grated

Method

- Peel and cut the potatoes into 3cm chunks then place in a saucepan full of cold water - do not rinse them.
- Add the salt and the whole peeled cloves of garlic to the water and bring to the boil, reducing it to simmer until the potatoes are soft enough for a sharp knife to pierce through.
- Drain the potatoes and garlic fully using a colander.
- Using a potato ricer, puree the cooked potato and garlic back into the dry saucepan with the butter.

- Place the saucepan over a low heat and stir the potato mixture to mix the butter and garlic thoroughly. A silicon spatula is best for this so that sides and corners can be scraped as well.
- Slowly add the crème fraiche, stirring all the time over a low heat to develop a creamy sticky texture.
- Still over the low heat, add the grated cheese, a small amount at a time, incorporating each amount before adding the next.
- It is ready when is is thick and silky and makes long strands when the spatula is lifted up.

Recommended Cheeses

Despite its roots being in France, there are now a number of cheesemakers in Britain producing a Tomme style cheese and some of the recommended ones are…
Tommie (CTV Cheese on the Wey), Rainton Tomme (CUVO Ethical Dairy), Moorland Tomme (CUVO Botton Creamery), Bevistan Tomme (SPV Bevistan Dairy)

Options

- Other Alpine style cheeses could be used as alternatives as they have the same stretchy qualities at Tomme (see page 75 *'Chrosti'* recipe for other Alpine cheeses)

Ulster Blue Potato Cake

The potato cake is a traditional and much loved food in Ireland and forms a key part of the Ulster Fry. This variation takes this iconic breakfast item and incorporates one of the delicious blue cheeses made in Ulster. Although its roots are as a breakfast dish, it can be served as a side dish to any meal.

Ingredients

Makes 6 potato cakes

- 250g cold mashed potato
- 4 spring onions - finely chopped
- 1 large eggs - beaten
- Salt and pepper for seasoning
- 100g plain flour
- 75g blue cheese - crumbled
- 30ml rapeseed oil

Method

- Mix the mashed potato and the spring onions together in a large bowl.
- Add the beaten egg and 75g of the flour to the potato and mix well.
- Add salt and pepper seasoning to taste.
- Crumble the blue cheese into the mixture and mix well.
- Sprinkle the remaining 25g of flour onto a cool worktop.

- When the mixture has formed a dough-like consistency remove it from the bowl and place onto the floured worktop.
- Divide the dough into 6 pieces and roll each into a ball, then flatten with the palm of your hand to form a cake about 2cm thick.
- Heat the oil in a frying pan and fry the cakes for about 10 minutes each side until they are golden brown and crispy

Recommended Cheeses

Given the inspiration of Northern Ireland for this recipe, it makes sense to use an Ulster made cheese. There are three that are particularly suitable for this…

Young Buck (CUA Mike's Fancy Cheeses), Sperrin Blue (CPV Dart Mountain), Kearney Blue (CPA Farmview Dairies), Meeny Hill Blue (CPV Dart Mountain)

Options

- If you don't like blue cheese, there are other excellent cheeses made in Northern Ireland that can be substituted but make sure it can be mixed into the potato mixture easily.

Ginny's Y³ Yorkshire Yorkshire Yorkshires

This recipe is a twist on traditional Yorkshire puddings but with added Wensleydale cheese to give a delicious tanginess. Gravy made with Yorkshire wine gives it the third Y. Named after a good friend who suggested the original name for this book, her 'prize' was to have a recipe named for her. The fact that she lives in Yorkshire is purely a happy coincidence.

Ingredients

Makes 8 puddings

- 30g salted butter
- 1 small onion - finely chopped
- 1 chicken stock cube - crumbled
- 2 tsp dried sage
- 100 ml white wine from Yorkshire
- 150g cream cheese
- 30ml rapeseed oil
- 100g plain flour
- 1 egg - beaten
- 150ml milk
- 100g Wensleydale - grated

Method

- Melt the butter in a saucepan and add the chopped onion and cook over a low heat for 10 minutes until they have softened but not browned.
- Add the crumbled stock cube and dried sage and cook for 5 minutes.
- Add the white wine and bring to the boil stirring continuously then lower heat to a gentle simmer for about 10 minutes until reduced by half.
- Add the cream cheese and cook over a low heat for 5 minutes stirring all the time until it reaches the desired thickness. Remove from the heat and only reheat when required for the puddings.
- Use the oil to coat a 6 hole muffin tin and place into an oven at 200°C/180°C Fan/Gas Mark 6. *It is very important that the tin is piping hot.*
- Add the beaten egg then gradually add the milk, whisking constantly until it is a smooth batter then leave it to rest for at least 30 minutes.
- Re-whisk the batter and add half the cheese, mixing well into the batter.
- Remove the hot muffin tin from the oven and quickly divide the cheesy batter between the holes, before placing it back in the oven immediately.
- After 10 minutes remove the muffin tin and sprinkle the remaining cheese onto the puddings before placing back into the oven for a

further 10 - 15 minutes until they have risen and are a medium golden brown.
- Remove from the oven and serve with the gravy poured into the puddings.

Recommended Cheeses
Clearly this recipe needs cheeses from Yorkshire
Airedale (CPV Eldwick Creamery), Fellstone (CUA Whin Yeats),
Fallen Monk (SUV Lacey's), Yorkshire Pecorino (SPA Yorkshire Pecorino)

Recommended Wines
Despite its northerly latitude, Yorkshire makes some really good wines, especially whites…
Laurel Vines Solaris, Dunesforde Pinot Gris, Ryedale Yorkshire's Lass, Yorkshire Heart Winemaker's Choice

Options
- Although considered sacrilege in Yorkshire, either Lancashire or Cheshire would prove a worthy replacement for the local cheeses.

Giant Yummy Beans

Nearly everybody loves baked beans but this recipe take them to a whole new level. Massive beans and massive flavours make them a sure fire favourite, served as either a side dish or on toast as a snack at any time of day.

Ingredients

Serves 4 people

- 2 teaspoons rapeseed oil
- 1 shallot - finely diced
- 2 cloves of garlic - crushed
- 4 rashers smoked streaky bacon - diced
- 2 tablespoons tomato purée
- 1 tin chopped tomatoes
- 2 tins butter beans
- 1 teaspoon smoked paprika
- 1 teaspoon ground cumin
- Salt and pepper for seasoning
- 100g strong cheese - grated

Method

- In a medium saucepan, cook the diced shallot over a low heat in the rapeseed oil for about 5 minutes until soft but not coloured.

- Add the crushed garlic and diced bacon and cook for 5 more minutes, stirring regularly, until the bacon has started to brown lightly.
- Stir in the tomato purée and cook it for 2 minutes before adding the chopped tomatoes and butter beans with their juice and stir well to mix.
- Add the smoked paprika, ground cumin and salt and pepper to taste.
- NB - if you prefer your beans a bit spicier, add more smoked paprika to taste.
- Simmer for about 20 minutes, stirring regularly until the sauce has thickened then add the grated cheese and stir until it has melted into the beans.
- Cook for a further 5 minutes to allow the flavours to combine.

Recommended Cheeses

There are a number of suitable cheeses but the best results come from using strongly flavoured easily grated or crumbled cheeses such as…

Lord of the Hundreds (SUV Traditional Cheese Dairy), Auld Lochnagar (CUA Cambus O'May), Bermondsey Hard Pressed (CUAO Kappacasein), Little Hereford (CUV Monkland Cheese)

Options
- For a vegetarian version, simply leave out the bacon.

Lincolnshire Roasted Sprouts

Probably one of the most controversial of vegetables, there is a saying that everything is improved by melting cheese over it and that is certainly the case here. Whether you are a sprout lover or not, you will enjoy this tasty side dish. Given that Lincolnshire is one of the largest sprout growing regions in the country, it seemed appropriate to use two cheeses from the farmhouse artisan cheesemakers in the county (Cote Hill Farm and Lincolnshire Poacher Cheese).

Ingredients

Serves 6 people

- 500g Brussels sprouts
- 1 tablespoon rapeseed oil
- 25g unsalted butter
- Pinch of salt and ground black pepper
- 100g British crème fraiche (recommend using full fat version)
- 1 teaspoon nutmeg (recommend freshly grated)
- 75g Cote Hill Red - grated
- 75g Lincolnshire Poacher - grated
- 50g fresh breadcrumbs

Method

- Remove any damaged or yellow outer leaves from the sprouts.
- Trim the base of the sprouts and cut them in half through the base.

- Cook the sprout halves in the rapeseed oil and butter and salt and pepper seasoning in a frying pan for 5 minutes turning regularly until lightly browned.
- Tip the sprouts into an ovenproof roasting dish.
- Warm the crème fraiche, but don't let it boil, in the same frying pan.
- Add the grated nutmeg to the crème fraiche
- Add 50g of each of the cheeses to the crème fraiche and stir until melted.
- Pour the cheese sauce over the sprouts, stirring and coating them.
- Sprinkle the remaining 25g of each of the cheeses over the top.
- Sprinkle the breadcrumbs over the top.
- Cook in an oven preheated to 200°C/180°C Fan/Gas Mark 6 for 20 minutes until lightly browned.

Recommended Cheeses

The key for this recipe is to use Lincolnshire cheeses, both of which are made on the farm using milk from their own cows and their Alpine style cheeses have the depth of flavour and melting qualities needed to make this tasty and satisfying dish.

Cote Hill Red (CUV Cote Hill), Lincolnshire Poacher (CUA Lincolnshire Poacher)

Options

- Other Alpine style cheeses could be substituted (see page 75 'Chrosti' recipe for other Alpine cheeses)

Northampton Beer Cobblers

There are many definitions of a *cobbler*, but the one used here is a scone like topping used on savoury casserole type dishes. In this recipe, cheese has been added to boost the flavour and the *cobblers* can be used as a side accompaniment for any dish but would work particularly well alongside a Chilli Con Carne or similar spicy dish. The name is really a play on words as the traditional shoe making industry of Northampton led to *Cobblers* being adopted as the nickname for the local football team. Beer is used in the recipe and although pretty much any full bodied beer could be used, the use of a Northampton made beer from Phipps NBC adds to the story of this recipe.

Ingredients

Makes 8 cobblers

- 150g self-raising flour plus small amount for dusting surface
- 15g baking powder
- 100g salted butter - cold from the fridge
- 100g cheese - grated
- 1 egg - beaten
- 2 teaspoons creamed horseradish
- 150ml beer (approx)
- 25ml rapeseed oil - for oiling baking parchment

Method

- Coarsely grate the cold butter, quickly to avoid it melting, then return to the fridge to chill down again.
- Mix the flour, baking powder and the cold cubed butter in a food processor or using fingers until it has the consistency of fine breadcrumbs.
- Place the flour mixture in a large bowl, add and mix the grated cheese.
- Mix the beaten egg and creamed horseradish and mix well into the flour and butter mixture.
- Slowly add the beer to the bowl stirring to form a dough. You may not need all of the beer to form a soft dough, making sure it isn't too wet.
- Tip the dough out onto a floured surface and mould together as one ball.
- Divide the dough into 8 small handful sized pieces of dough and roll them into balls, then flatten each of them into a thick disc.
- Place the discs onto a sheet of oiled baking parchment on a baking tray.
- Cook in an oven preheated to 200°C/180°C Fan/Gas Mark 6 for 15 - 20 minutes until lightly browned.

Recommended Cheeses

There are only two cheesemakers in Northamptonshire and they both make cheeses that would work well in this recipe…

Cobblers Nibble (CUV Hamm Tun), Phipps Firkin (CPVO Northamptonshire Cheese), Tongue Taster (CPVO Northamptonshire Cheese)

Recommended Beers

All of these beers are made by Phipps NBC in the centre of Northampton…

Becket's Honey Ale, Midsummer Meadow, Gold Star, Solar Star

Options

- English mustard can be used instead of horseradish to give a different but equally punchy flavour.

Blue Goat Mushrooms

Many people assume all goat's cheese is made as a soft white cheese, usually log or pyramid shaped, without ever being aware that blue goat's cheese is also made. The tanginess of the blue combined with the acid freshness of the goat's cheese makes it an ideal partner for the earthy richness of chestnut mushrooms.

Ingredients

Serves 4 people

- *20* chestnut mushrooms
- 1 red onion
- 20ml rapeseed oil
- 2 cloves garlic - grated or crushed
- 200g blue goat's cheese
- 20g unsalted butter

Method

- Remove the stalks from mushrooms and dice the stalks finely.
- Finely dice the red onion and cook it gently in rapeseed oil until softened but not browned.
- Add the chopped mushroom stalks and the grated garlic to the pan and cook for a further 5 minutes.
- When the mushrooms and onions have softened and lightly browned remove from heat.
- Crumble the cheese into the still warm pan and stir well to mix.

- Fill the mushroom caps with the mixture and dot each one with a small knob of butter.
- Place the mushrooms cap side down in a shallow roasting dish and cook in an oven preheated to 200°C/180°C Fan/Gas Mark 6 for 15 minutes until the stuffing is bubbling and lightly browned.

Recommended Cheeses
There are not many blue goat's cheeses made in Britain, but those that are demonstrate the tangy flavour of this style of cheese…
Cornish Nanny (GPV Cornish Cheese), Harbourne Blue (GPV Ticklemore Dairy), Biggar Blue (GUV Errington Cheese), Nanny Blue (GPV Teesdale Cheesemakers)

Options
- Instead of a blue goat's cheese, but any blue cheese could be used as a substitute.
- For the blue cheese haters, any other crumbly cheese could be used, such as a Cheshire, Lancashire or Wensleydale.

Goat's Cheese Nuggets

These nuggets of chunks of mixed vegetables are given an extra bite by the addition of tangy goat's cheese.

Ingredients
Makes 20 nuggets
- 20g salted butter
- 250g broccoli florets
- 250g cauliflower florets
- 100g carrots
- 100g courgette
- 50g fresh breadcrumbs
- 1 egg
- Pinch of salt and ground black pepper
- 200g goat's cheese - crumbled
- 4 spring onions - finely chopped

Method
- Use the butter to grease a baking tray.
- Lower the broccoli and cauliflower florets into boiling water for 3 minutes, drain and blanche by immediately plunging them into a bowl of iced water.
- After 3 minutes in the iced water, drain and chop into small pieces about 1 cm across.
- Peel and grate the carrots using a large hole box grater.

- Peel and grate the courgettes using a large hole box grater and squeeze dry.
- Mix the chopped and grated vegetables in a large bowl.
- Add the crumbled goat's cheese and spring onions and mix again.
- Add fresh breadcrumbs, egg and salt and pepper seasoning to the bowl and mix well.
- Roll heaped tablespoon quantities of the mixture into nugget shapes and place the nuggets on the buttered baking tray.
- Cook in an oven preheated to 200°C/180°C Fan/Gas Mark 6 for 15 minutes, turn them over and cook for 15 minutes more.
- The nuggets are cooked when they are golden brown and crispy

Recommended Cheeses

There are some truly excellent goat's cheeses made in Britain today and some fine examples are recommended for this recipe…

Rosary (GPV Rosary), Perroche (GPV Neal's Yard Creamery),
Ailsa Craig (GPV Dunlop Dairy), Curthwaite (GUV Thornby Moor)

Options

- For anyone who dislikes goat's cheese or fancies something different, a medium strength Cheddar can be substituted.

Sweet Dishes

Wensleydale, Ginger and Rhubarb Crumble

A variation of a traditional fruit crumble by using crumbly Wensleydale combined with rhubarb in this Yorkshire influenced recipe. The combination of crystallised ginger and Wensleydale was used in my first book 'British Cheese on Toast' and adds a tangy taste sensation.

Although Wensleydale is a traditional Yorkshire cheese, there are some fine examples of artisan dales style cheese made in neighbouring counties as well.

NB - using locally made real honey supports local beekeepers and also gives a better result than commercially produced sugar adulterated honey.

Ingredients

Serves 6 people

- 350g rhubarb - about 8 medium stalks - trimmed and cut into 4 cm lengths
- 50ml honey
- 75g plain flour
- 75g porridge oats
- 75g demerara sugar
- 75g cold unsalted butter - cut into small cubes
- 75g crystallised ginger - cut into small pieces
- 100g Wensleydale cheese - crumbled

Method

- Lay the rhubarb into an ovenproof dish, in two layers if needed.
- Drizzle the honey over the rhubarb covering as much as possible.
- Place in the oven at 200°C/180°C Fan/Gas Mark 6 for 15 minutes until the rhubarb has softened then remove and allow to cool a little.
- To make the crumble topping, mix the flour, oats and sugar in a large bowl then rub in the cold butter using finger tips until the mixture resembles breadcrumbs.
- Spread the chopped ginger over the top of the slightly cooled rhubarb then spread the crumbled cheese over the top.
- Spread the crumble topping over the top making sure it is covering evenly and press down very lightly.
- Cook in the oven at 200°C/180°C Fan/Gas Mark 6 for 30 minutes until the crumble is golden brown and crispy.

Recommended Cheeses

Amongst the cheese that work well in this recipe are…

Yoredale (CUAV Curlew Dairy), Stonebeck (CUA Stonebeck Dairy), Swaledale (CPV Swaledale Cheese), Kit Calvert Wensleydale (CPV Wensleydale Creamery)

Options

- Not everyone likes rhubarb so as an alternative it can be replaced by pear cut into quarters.

Lancashire Fruit Cake Parcels

I am sure it would be a much better world if everyone made their own pastry, fruit cake and apple sauce but as this book is about simple recipes, why not use ready made versions? Life is just too short and you want to be enjoying these warm tasty parcels as fast as possible, so just buy ready made, unless of course you are a serious home chef and want to make your own.

Lancashire cheese is made in two traditional and one modern style. *Creamy* is a young fresh cheese matured for only a few months, whereas *Tasty* is matured for up to 6 months giving a more robust flavour. *Crumbly* is a newer style, created to be made quickly and matured in weeks. It is personal taste as to which style you choose to use, but it is recommended to use one made in Lancashire in the traditional method.

Ingredients

Makes 4 parcels

- 1 sheet ready made chilled puff pastry 350mm x 230mm (350g)
- Plain flour - for dusting surface
- 120g rich dark fruit cake - cut into 5cm squares approx 1cm thick
- 100g Lancashire cheese
- 4 teaspoons apple sauce
- 1 egg - beaten

Method

- Thaw the chilled pastry then roll out onto a lightly floured worktop.
- Cut the pastry into 6 squares by cutting in half along the length and into three across the width. Each square should be just under 12cm.
- Place the fruit cake squares in the centre of the pastry squares in a diamond formation (points facing the side of the square).
- Place a 25g slice of Lancashire on top of the fruitcake and spread one teaspoon of the apple sauce over the cheese.
- Brush some of the beaten egg over the exposed corners of the pastry and then fold the corners to the centre getting the points to meet as closely as possible. If there is a small hole remaining it really doesn't matter.
- Brush the remaining egg over the parcels and place them on a sheet of baking parchment on a try in the oven at 200°C/180°C Fan/Gas Mark 6 for about 20 minutes until they are crisp and golden.

Recommended Cheeses

As mentioned in the introduction to the recipe, which style you use a matter of personal taste, but the following are recommended…
Mrs Kirkham's (CUA Mrs Kirkham's), Beacon Fell (CPV Dewlay), Sunday Best (CPV Butler's), Greenfields (CPV Greenfields)

Options

- Although considered sacrilege in Lancashire, a suitable replacement cheese would be Wensleydale or Cheshire.

Blue Cheese and Chocolate Hobnobs

This is possibly one of the most unusual recipes in this book, in fact not really a recipe at all but an assembly of three ingredients in a perfect pairing. The pairing works on a flavour and textural level with the salty cheese and sweet wine complementing each other and the soft cheese and crumbly oats in the Hobnob contrasting well. Despite using blue cheese it is even enjoyed by many previously confirmed blue cheese haters.

There are plenty of recipes for homemade Hobnobs online, but consistent with the theme of this book, why would you when the bought ones are so good and also so much easier.

Ingredients

Makes one Hobnob (warning, this will not be enough)

- 1 dark chocolate Hobnob
- 25g soft creamy blue cheese
- 1 small glass of sweet wine (you decide how small)

Method

- Spread the blue cheese on top of the chocolate side of the Hobnob.
- Enjoy it with the wine.

Recommended Cheeses

The key for this recipe is to use a soft spreadable milder blue cheese…

Kingcott Blue (CUV Kingcott Dairy), Cornish Blue (CPV Cornish Cheese), Barkham Blue (CPV Village Maid Cheese), Leeds Blue (SPA Yorkshire Pecorino)

Recommended Wines

Sweet wines are still unusual for British vineyards but those that are made are worth seeking out…

Biddenden Schönburger, Eglantine North Star, Hattingley Valley Entice

Options

- The original and best recipe uses Hobnobs, but this idea also works using Jammie Dodgers - yes really, try it for yourself!

Snacks & Nibbles

Sheep, Pear, Honey

This is so simple that it is more of a combination than a recipe. It is a dish that was hugely popular on the menu of the cheese shop and wine bar. The tangy bite of a hard sheep's cheese, paired with the acidic sweetness and juiciness of the pear all brought together by the sticky natural sweetness of honey makes for a tasty light snack. The dish is ideal when served with fresh crusty bread to soak up the mixed juices.

NB - using locally made real honey supports local beekeepers and also gives a better result than commercially produced sugar adulterated honey.

Ingredients

Serves one person as a light snack

- ½ pear - thinly sliced lengthwise
- 75g hard sheep's cheese - thinly sliced
- 25g honey

Method

- Lay the pear slices on the base of a small overproof dish.
- Lay the sheep's cheese slices over the top of the pear.
- Cover the dish with tin foil.
- Place in an oven at 200°C/180°C Fan/Gas Mark 6 for about 10 minutes.

- Remove the foil to check the cheese is bubbling slightly around the edges.
- Drizzle the honey over the top and serve.

Recommended Cheeses

The best cheeses to use in this dish are hard sheep's cheeses and there are some great examples made in Britain…

Hardy's (SPV Book & Bucket), Corra Linn (SUA Errington Cheese), Spenwood (STV Village Maid), Duddleswell (SPV High Weald)

Options

- If you prefer not to use sheep's cheese, any hard goat's or cow's milk cheese would be an acceptable substitute.

Goat, Mango, Marmalade

This is similar to the previous recipe in its simplicity but totally different in its components. This time the acidity of the hard goats's cheese works together with the lusciousness and freshness of the mango and the sweet acidity of the marmalade. The dish is great served with fresh crusty bread to soak up the mixed juices.

Ingredients

Serves one person as a light snack

- 75g mango thinly sliced
- 75g hard goat's cheese - thinly sliced
- 40g marmalade

Method

- Lay the mango slices on the base of a small overproof dish.
- Lay the goat's cheese slices over the top of the mango.
- Cover the dish with tin foil.
- Place in an oven at 200°C/180°C Fan/Gas Mark 6 for about 10 minutes.
- Remove the foil to check the cheese is bubbling slightly around the edges.
- Spoon the marmalade over the top and serve.

Recommended Cheeses

The best cheeses to use in this dish are hard goat's cheeses and there are some great examples made in Britain…

Rachel (GTV White Lake), Bonnington Linn (GUA Errington Cheese), Quicke's Goat (GPV Quicke's), Kelly's Canterbury Goat (GUV Cheesemakers of Canterbury)

Options

- If you prefer not to use goats cheese, any hard sheep's or cow's milk cheese would be an acceptable substitute.
- As an alternative to mango, any firm fruit such as a nectarine or a pear can be used instead.
- Marmalade can be replaced by honey if preferred.

Blue Breadcakes

Soda bread is a traditional form of bread using baking powder and soda to make it rise, without using any yeast. This version is enhanced by the use of
blue cheese to give it a tangy flavour and also honey to balance out the tanginess. The addition of the cheese and the honey produces something that is halfway between a bread and a cake, hence the unusual (and made up) name for this recipe..

NB - using locally made real honey supports local beekeepers and also gives a better result than commercially produced sugar adulterated honey.

Ingredients

Makes 12 breadcakes

- 150g plain flour
- 125g wholemeal flour
- 1½ teaspoon baking powder
- ½ teaspoon bicarbonate of soda
- 70g salted butter - cold from the fridge
- 200g blue cheese - crumbled
- 1 egg
- 75g plain yogurt
- 75ml semi-skimmed milk
- 25ml honey

Method

- Cut 60g of the cold butter into small cubes, quickly to avoid it melting, then return to the fridge to chill down again.
- Mix 125g of the plain flour, all of the wholemeal flour, baking powder and bicarbonate in a large bowl then add the cold cubed butter.
- Mix the flour and butter with a fork until it resembles coarse sand.
- Crumble the blue cheese into the bowl and mix well using fingers to break up the cheese if required.
- Gently mix the egg, yogurt, milk and honey together in another bowl and then stir into the flour mixture but do not mix too much so that the air is retained in the mixture.
- Use 10g butter to grease 12 cups in a muffin tin then sprinkle the remaining 25g plain flour all over the butter to cover the muffin tin cups.
- Spoon the dough into the tin and spread it out to the edges.
- Place in an oven at 200°C/180°C Fan/Gas Mark 6 for 45 minutes. Check that the breadcakes have risen and have a crusty top. Test by poking a sharp knife into the centre and checking it is clean when pulled out.
- Let them cool before tipping them out of the tin.

Recommended Cheeses

The nature of this recipe needs the tanginess of blue cheese because anything milder will not be tasted...

Stow Blue (CPV Cotswold Cheese), Buffalo Blue (BPV Shepherd's Purse), Shoetown Blue (CUV Hamm Tun), Dovedale Blue (CPV Staffordshire Cheese)

Options

- If blue cheese is not to your liking, another crumbly cheese such as Cheshire, Wensleydale or Caerphilly can be substituted.

West Country Dip

This hot dip is made using ingredients typically associated with the west of England, hence the name. It could almost be described as a thick fondue but is designed as a either snack or a starter for a meal.

Ingredients

Makes a large bowl suitable for 4 people

- 1 clove garlic
- 200g West Country cheddar - grated
- 20g unsalted butter
- 50ml dry cider

For dipping

- Toast soldiers or fingers
- Vegetable crudités - dipping sized pieces of carrots, celery, cauliflower, red/green peppers, asparagus,

Method

- Finely grate the garlic to a paste.
- Add the crushed garlic, grated cheddar, butter and cider to a food processor.
- Blitz until a smooth paste is formed.
- Spoon the dip into a small saucepan and warm whilst stirring.
- Pour into a serving bowl.
- Dip crudités or toast into the dip or spread on slices of toast.

Recommended Cheeses

There are many different cheddars from the West Country so chose your own favourite…

Quicke's (CPAV Quicke's), Green's Twanger (CPV Green's of Glastonbury), Times Past Traditional (CPV Times Past Dairy), Lye Cross Mature (CPV Lye Cross)

Options

- For an alcohol free version, replace the cider with a quality apple juice.

Double Gloucester Bakes

Double Gloucester is one of the great territorial cheeses of Britain, but whose reputation has unfortunately been spoiled by commercially made versions using the name, but without the tradition or heritage. These simple to make and very tasty nibbles use this cheese and it is highly recommended to use a traditionally made version from the county of Gloucestershire.

Ingredients
Makes 20 - 24 bakes
- 120g plain flour
- 75g Double Gloucester - grated
- 85g unsalted butter - chilled
- 1 egg - beaten

Method
- Mix 100g of the flour and grated cheese in a bowl.
- Cut 75g of the chilled butter into small cubes and rub it into the flour mix with fingertips until the mixture is like fine breadcrumbs.
- Add the beaten egg to the mixture and mix with hands to form a dough.
- Place the dough on a lightly floured surface and mould it into a log shape.
- Roll the log to 25cm long and wrap it in waxed paper.
- Chill in the fridge for an hour.

- Use the remaining 10g of the butter to grease a flat baking tray.
- Cut the chilled dough into 1cm thick slices and place on the buttered baking tray.
- Place in a preheated oven at 200°C/180°C Fan/Gas Mark 6 for 10 minutes until they are a golden colour.
- Remove and cool on a wire rack.

Recommended Cheeses

As the name of the recipe suggests, a Double Gloucester cheese is required and it is better to use a traditional version made in Gloucestershire....

Martell's Double Gloucester (CUPV Charles Martell),

Smart's Double Gloucester (CUV Smart's),

Daylesford Double Gloucester (CPAO Daylesford Organics),

Jonathan Crump's Double Gloucester (CUV Jonathan Crump's)

Options

- Although Double Gloucester is preferred, Single Gloucester or Red Leicester can be substituted.

Single Gloucester Crisps

Simple to make, tasty and very popular as a nibble with drinks. They could be made with a number of different cheeses, but trials have shown that the combination of flavour and texture of a traditionally made Single Gloucester is ideal for these thin crisps. The production of Single Gloucester is regulated by a Protected Designation of Origin stipulating that it must be made in the county using milk from a herd containing Gloucester cows. Accordingly, the number of dairies producing this traditional cheese are limited. Traditionally the cheese was made as lesser cheese to Double Gloucester not good enough to be sent out of the county and was only for local farm workers.

Ingredients

Makes 20 - 24 crisps

- 100g Single Gloucester - finely grated
- 2 teaspoons plain flour
- Pinch of black pepper

Method

- Mix all the ingredients together in a bowl.
- Place a tablespoon of the mixture in a pile on a sheet of baking parchment on top of a baking tray.
- Flatten the pile into a thin round disc.
- Repeat leaving space between the discs.

- Bake in an oven preheated to 200°C/180°C Fan/Gas Mark 6 for 5 - 10 minutes until golden and bubbling.
- Use a palette knife to transfer the crisps to a cooling rack.

Recommended Cheeses

Traditionally made artisan Single Gloucester is only made by a few cheesemakers…

Godsell's Single Gloucester (CPV Godsell's),
Greystones Single Gloucester (CPVO Simon Weaver Organic),
Daylesford Single Gloucester (CPAO Daylesford Organics),
Jonathan Crump' Single Gloucesters (CUV Jonathan Crump's)

Options

- As an alternative to Single Gloucester, other cheeses that would prove suitable would be Double Gloucester or a Red Leicester.

Yeasty Cheesy Puffs

The combination of Cheddar and yeast extract is an umami explosion that is loved and hated in equal measure. Assuming that either you or your audience are lovers, this simple recipe will delight the lovers. The haters will just have to have something else!

Ingredients

Makes 20 puffs

- 100g unsalted butter
- 250ml water
- 1 tablespoon yeast extract
- 125g plain flour
- 4 large eggs
- 125g Cheddar - grated

Method

- Mix the butter, water and yeast extract in a saucepan and boil.
- Lower the heat, add the flour and stir well.
- Stir until the dough forms a ball then stir for another three minutes.
- Allow to cool until the dough is warm not hot.
- Beat the eggs one at a time and add to the dough stirring each one in before adding the next one.
- The dough should form a creamy texture.
- Stir in the grated cheddar.

- Using a tablespoon, shape the mixture into balls and place on a sheet of baking parchment on top of a baking tray. Ensure there is a space between each ball.
- Bake in an oven preheated to 200°C/180°C Fan/Gas Mark 6 for 30 minutes until golden and puffed up.

Recommended Cheeses

Due to the strong flavour of the yeast extract, it is important to have a full flavour cheese in this recipe…

Wyfe of Bath (CPVO Bath Soft Cheese Co), Weardale (CPV Weardale Cheese), Guernsleigh Original (CPV Guernsleigh), Leonard Stanley (CPV Godsells)

Options

- There are a number of brands of yeast extract made in Britain, of which Marmite is probably the best known but own brand versions or Australian made Vegemite could be used.

Spicy Cheese Scrunchies

These scrunchies were so named by my wife upon first tasting them. They are soft in the centre with a slightly crunchy outside, full of flavour and ideal nibbles to serve with drinks. The quantities of paprika, herbs and garlic give a strong taste so feel free to adjust them if you prefer something milder.

Ingredients

Makes 20 Scrunchies

- 120g plain flour
- 1 tablespoon baking powder
- 2 teaspoons paprika
- 3 teaspoons mixed dried herbs - choose from parsley, sage, thyme, basil
- 2 teaspoons garlic granules or powder
- 100g unsalted butter - diced
- 125g cheddar - grated
- 2 teaspoons extra virgin cold-pressed rapeseed oil
- 3 tablespoons cold water

Method

- Mix 100g of the flour, baking powder, paprika, dried herbs and garlic granules or powder in a large bowl

- Add the butter and cheese and mix until the dough forms a ball. This can be done either by using fingers or with the blade in a food processor.
- Add the oil and water and mix to form a soft dough.
- Wrap the dough and chill it in the fridge for 30 minutes.
- Roll the dough out on a lightly floured surface to 4mm thickness and cut into 2cm squares.
- Place the squares on a sheet of baking parchment on top of a baking tray ensuring there is a space between each square.
- Bake in an oven preheated to 200°C/180°C Fan/Gas Mark 6 for 10 - 15 minutes until golden and crisp.

Recommended Cheeses

Given the strength of flavours in this recipe, a stronger tasting cheese is required and a commercially produced Cheddar is recommended…

Barber's 1833 Vintage Reserve (CPV Barber's), Seriously Strong Vintage (CPV Caledonian Creamery), Colliers Powerful (CPV Fayrefield Foods), Cathedral City Vintage (CPV Davidstow Creamery)

Options

- Paprika, garlic and herbs can be replaced by any spices or seasonings of your choice.

Cheshire Flapjack

For many people, the best biscuits to enjoy with their cheese are oat crackers. Oats are rich in fibre, low in GI, fat and cholesterol so provide a nutritious base for these tasty snacks. Flapjack is generally considered to be a sweet snack, but this version is made with cheese, sage and onion to give a classic savoury flavour. Given that flapjack was first mentioned in a Shakespearean play, it seems appropriate to use one of the country's oldest known cheeses, Cheshire, in this recipe.

Ingredients

Makes 20 pieces

- 60g unsalted butter - softened
- 150g Cheshire - grated
- 150g rolled porridge oats
- ½ onion - finely diced
- 2 eggs
- 1 teaspoon dried sage

Method

- Preheat the oven to 200°C/180°C Fan/Gas Mark 6.
- Use 10g of butter to grease a 20cm shallow baking tray.
- Mix 50g of butter together with the remaining ingredients in a bowl.

- Press the mixture into the baking tray using a knife to smooth it over.
- Bake in the oven for 30 minutes until golden brown.
- Cool and cut into bite size pieces.

Recommended Cheeses

A number of different cheeses could be used but the recommendation is for a traditionally made artisan Cheshire, which is made by only a few cheesemakers (East Lee is a Cheshire/Lancashire style)…

Appleby's (CUA Appleby's), Mrs Bourne's (CPV Mrs Bourne's), East Lee (CPVO Pextenement Cheese), Belton Farm (CPV Belton Farm)

Options

- Other crumbly northern cheeses such as Lancashire or Wensleydale can be used in place of Cheshire.

Frozen Blue Cheese Dust

This is not a recipe, but a surprising and very tasty suggestion. It is advised to keep a small piece of blue cheese in the freezer permanently so that you can produce this taste sensation at a moment's notice.

Ingredients
- Small piece of any blue cheese

Method
- Place a small piece of the chosen blue cheese in the freezer, wrapped in waxed paper until it is totally frozen. This is ideally done a day in advance.
- Remove the frozen cheese and using a very fine grater or a microplane, grate the cheese as a dust over a plate of charcuterie as a seasoning.
- NB - this works particularly well with stronger flavoured charcuterie such as Bresaola (air-dried beef, Finocchiona (fennel salami) or Spianate Calabrese (spicy salami).

Recommended Cheeses

Pretty much any blue cheese can be used as long as it isn't too soft and creamy. There are a number of blue cheeses that you may not have tried which are well worth seeking out…

Blue Millie (CTV Cheese on the Wey), Blue Bay (CPV Country Cheeses), Norbury Blue (CUV Norbury Park Farm), Pevensey Blue (CPA Pevensey Cheese)

Options

- Although this is recommended for use with charcuterie it can be equally effective and tasty with other cold foods such as salad, chicken or vegetables.

  It is not advisable to use with hot food as the dust will melt!

Rocks and Honey

This is so incredibly simple that it hardly counts as a recipe, but so incredibly tasty that it is a guaranteed hit whenever it is served. It can be used as a innovative canapé or served as a palate cleanser between courses, or even as a mini-dessert. The combination of a salty tangy brittle texture with a smooth luxurious sweet contrast is a truly wonderful delight for the senses.

NB - using locally made real honey supports local beekeepers and also gives a better result than commercially produced sugar adulterated honey.

Ingredients

Serves 2 people

- 100g hard brittle cheese
- 50ml runny honey

Method

- Using a sharp knife, break the cheese into small lumps about 1cm in diameter.
- Pour the honey into a small bowl.
- Using either cocktail sticks or fingers, dip the cheese into the honey and pop it into your mouth…mmmm.

Recommended Cheeses

The cheese must be very hard and brittle so that it will break into lumps and some great examples are…

Old Winchester (CPV Lyburn Farmhouse), Cornish Kern (CPA Lynher Dairies), Knuckleduster (CUA Lincolnshire Poacher), Ancient Ashmore (CUV Cheesemakers of Canterbury)

Options

- There are a number of different flavour honeys dependent on where bees have gathered nectar from. Some of the most common styles are heather, clover and acacia. Try experimenting with different styles to get the flavour combination that you like best.
- This can also work well by dipping walnuts as well as cheese into the honey.

Thank You

I never know where to start when thanking the many people who have helped me create and publish a book and am always worried that I may miss out someone important, but here goes.

On a personal level, once again I have to thank my wife, Amanda, for sampling my cheese based cookery experiments and for helping me with proof-reading, editing and generally nonsense checking.

As always, my daughters who this book is dedicated to for being such great supporters (and cheese-eaters) and to their partners for supporting them.

My great friends in the north, Jonathan and Ginny McCloy, who are generous hosts for my various cheese journeys far from home and for kindly agreeing to taste and sample so many cheeses with me, always with excellent wines. Also to Ginny for coming up with the original title for the book itself.

Neighbours and good friends Ann Horsnell, Rowan Norbury, Ray Norbury and Courtenay Norbury, for spending many evenings around the table eating anything up to 6 different cheese based dishes that I am trialing and never complaining about the excess of cheese.

Chiswick Cheese Market (Cheesewick) which is held on the third Sunday of each month. It is organised and run by The Cookbook Kitchen, a team of brilliant lady chefs, food writers, caterers and all round lovely people. They all give their time and expertise freely to put on this incredible market showcasing a wide variety of cheesemakers, cheesemongers and sellers of all cheese related food and drink with the proceeds all being donated to charitable causes. I go every month because it is one of the best places to taste, sample, buy and continue to learn more about cheese.

The cheesemakers of Britain must be thanked for their tireless efforts and commitment to making the worlds best cheeses. Not only do they milk and tend to their herds and flocks, but they work long and thankless hours making and maturing their cheeses. Despite cheesemaking not being a very lucrative occupation with low and sometimes non-existent profit margins, I have been overwhelmed by their generosity in sending me samples of cheese to taste and use in recipes.

Any book needs a way of getting to the reader and I have to thank a number of cheesemongers, delicatessens and other quality shops for agreeing to stock and sell my previous books (and hopefully this one as well…)
Hampshire Deli & Cheeseshop, Cotswold Cheese Company, Attic, Hygge Cafe, Cheese at Leadenhall, Green & Lovely, No2 Pound St, Rippon Cheese, Pangbourne Cheese, Cheezelo, Norbury Park Farm, The Cheese Press, George & Joseph, Cheese on the Wey, The Artisan Collective, Sheldons Wine Merchants, The Cheese Hut.

Finally, to you, dear cheese eating reader. Thank you for reading my books and thank you for buying this one, unless it was a gift, in which case thank you to whoever bought it and thank you to you for reading it.

Thank you all.

Recommended Cheese Shops & Cheese Restaurants

Having worked for many years in the cheese business, as a retailer, wholesaler, restauranteur, consultant, cheese judge and writer, I have had the privilege and pleasure of visiting many superb cheese shops throughout Britain.

Whilst not purporting to be a comprehensive list, these are some of the cheese shops that I would highly recommend for their range of British cheeses, their knowledge and experience. I am sure there are many more fine cheese shops which I haven't had the pleasure of visiting, but this is my personal list arranged in alphabetical order.

& Caws www.andcaws.co.uk
1 Dale Street, Menai Bridge, Anglesey, LL59 5AL

Anderson & Hill www.andersonandhill.co.uk
7 Great Western Arcade, Birmingham, West Midlands, B2 5HU

Arcadia Delicatessen www.arcadiadeli.co.uk
378 Lisburn Road, Belfast, Antrim, BT9 6JL

Ashburton Delicatessen www.ashburtondelicatessen.co.uk
16 North Street, Ashburton, Devon, TQ13 7QD

The Artisan Cheesemonger www.theartisancheesemonger.com
40-42 High Street, Holywood, Down, BT18 9AD

Bakers and Larners of Holt www.bakersandlarnersco.uk
8 Market Place, Holt, Norfolk, Natural Rind25 6BW

Bayley & Sage www.bayley-sage.co.uk
- 141 Ebury Street, Belgravia, London
- 180-184 Fulham Road, Chelsea, London, SW10 9PN
- 835 Fulham Road, Fulham, London, SW6 5HQ
- 1-2 Lancer's Square, Kensington, London, W8 3EP
- 95 Northcote Road, Battersea, London, SW11 6PL
- 43-45 Parkgate Road, Battersea, London, SW11 4NP
- 30-34 New Kings Road, Parsons Green, London, SW6 4ST
- 33 Turnham Green Terrace, Turnham Green, London, W4 1RG
- 509 Old York Road, Wandsworth, London, SW18 1TF
- 660 High Street, Wimbledon Village, London, SW19 5EE

Birkdale Cheese Co www.birkdalecheese.com
- 42a Liverpool Road, Southport, Merseyside, PR8 4AY

Blacks Corner www.blackscorner.co.uk
- 1 St John's Terrace, East Boldon, South Tyneside, NE36 0LL

The Bristol Cheesemonger www.bristol-cheese.co.uk
- Unit 8, Cargo 2, Museum Street, Bristol, BS1 6ZA

Buchanan's www.buchananscheesemonger.com
- 5a Porchester Place, Connaught Village, London, W2 2BS

Calder Cheesehouse www.caldercheesehouse.com
- 56 Patmos, Burnley Road, Todmorden, West Yorkshire, OL14 5EY

The Cambridge Cheese Company www.cambridgecheese.com
- 4 All Saints Passage, Cambridge, Cambridgeshire, CB2 3LS

Cartmel Cheeses www.cartmelcheeses.co.uk
- 1 & 2 Unsworth's Yard, Cartmel, Cumbria, LA11 6PG

The Cheese and Wine Shop www.cheeseandwineshop.co.uk
- 8 Clark's Yard, Darlington, Durham, DL3 7QH

Cheese at Leadenhall www.cheeseatleadenhall.co.uk
🗀 4–5 Leadenhall Market, London, EC3V 1LR

Cheeses of Muswell Hill www.cheesesonline.co.uk
🗀 13 Fortis Green Road, Muswell Hill, London, N10 3HP

Cheese Etc www.cheese-etc.co.uk
🗀 17 Reading Road, Pangbourne, Berkshire, RG8 7LU

Cheese on the Green www.cheeseonthegreen.com
🗀 27 The Green, Bilton, Rugby, Warwickshire, CV22 7LZ

The Cheese Bar www.thecheesebar.com
🗀 Camden Stables Market, London, NW1 8AH

The Cheese Barge www.thecheesebar.com
🗀 Sheldon Square, Paddington Basin, London, W2 6DL

The Cheese Block www.instagram.com/thecheeseblockse22
🗀 69 Lordship Lane, East Dulwich, London, SE22 8EP

The Cheese Hamlet www.thecheesehamlet.co.uk
🗀 706 Wilmslow Road, Didsbury, Manchester, M20 2DW

Cheesegeek www.thecheesegeek.com
🗀 2 Station Approach, Raynes Park, London, SW20 0FT

The Cheese Hut www.thecheesehutshop.co.uk
🗀 1 Basin Road South, Portslade, East Sussex, BN41 1WF

The Cheese Lady www.thecheeselady.co.uk
🗀 3 Court Street, Haddington, East Lothian, EH41 3JD

The Cheese Locker www.thecheeselocker.com
🗀 High Ash, Goose Lane, Abbotts Bromley, Staffordshire, WS15 3DF

Cheese Louise   www.cheese-louise.co.uk
15 High Street, Alton, Hampshire, GU34 1FG

Cheese Please   www.cheesepleaselewes.co.uk
46 High Street, Lewes, East Sussex, BN7 2DD

The Cheese Press   www.thecheesepressrichmond.co.uk
7 Victoria Road, Richmond, North Yorkshire, DL10 4DW

The Cheese Shed   www.thecheeseshed.com
41 Fore Street, Bovey Tracey, Newton Abbot, Devon, TQ13 9AD

The Cheese Shop (Nottingham)   www.cheeseshopnottingham.co.uk
6 Flying Horse Walk, Nottingham, NG1 2HN

The Cheese Shop (Canterbury)   www.thecheeseshopcanterbury.co.uk
55 Palace Street, Canterbury, Kent, CT1 2DY

The Cheese Shop (Tunbridge Wells)   www.thecheeseshoptw.co.uk
48b St Johns Road, Tunbridge Wells, Kent, TN4 9NY

The Cheese Society   www.thecheesesociety.co.uk
1 St Martin's Lane, Lincoln, LN2 1HY

The Cheese Wheel   www.cheesewheel.uk
Torr Vale Mill, Torr Vale Road, New Mills, Derbyshire, SK22 3HS

The Cheese Yard   www.thecheeseyard.co.uk
69 King Street, Knutsford, Cheshire, WA16 6DX

The Cheeseboard of Harrogate   www.thecheeseboard.net
1 Commercial Street, Harrogate, North Yorkshire, HG1 1UB

The Cheesery   www.thecheesery.co.uk
9 Exchange Street, Dundee, DD1 3DJ

The Cheeseworks   www.thecheeseworks.co.uk
- 5 Regent Street, Cheltenham, Gloucestershire, GL50 1HE

Cheezelo   www.cheezelo.com
- 46 Chalton Street, Euston, London, NW1 1JB

Chiswick Cheese Market   www.chiswickcheesemarket.uk
- Old Market Place, Chiswick, London W4 2DR

Chorlton Cheesemongers   www.chorltoncheesemongers.co.uk
- 486 Wilbraham Road, Chorlton, Manchester, M21 9AS

The Cotswold Cheese Company   www.cotswoldcheese.com
- 5 High Street, Moreton-in-the-Marsh, Gloucestershire, GL56 0AH
- Digbeth Street, Stow on the Wold, Gloucestershire, GL54 1BN
- 113 High Street, Burford, Oxfordshire, OX18 4RG

Country Cheeses   www.countrycheeses.co.uk
- Market Road, Tavistock, Devon, PL19 0BW
- 26 Fore Street, Topsham, Devon, EX3 0HD
- 1 Ticklemore Street, Totnes, Devon, TQ9 5EJ

The Courtyard Dairy   www.thecourtyarddairy.co.uk
- Crows Nest Barn, Austwick, Settle, North Yorkshire, LA2 8A

Cryer and Stott   www.cryerandstott.co.uk
- 20 Market Place, Pontefract, West Yorkshire, WF8 1AU
- 31a Carlton Street, Castleford, West Yorkshire, WF10 1AL
- 25 Station Road, Allerton Bywater, Castleford, WF10 2BP

Darts Farm   www.dartsfarm.co.uk
- Darts Farm, Topsham, Devon, EX3 0QH

Daylesford Organic www.daylesford.com
- Daylesford, Near Kingham, Gloucestershire, GL56 0YG
- 76 - 82 Sloane Avenue, Brompton Cross, London, SW3 3DZ
- 208 - 212 Westbourne Grove, Notting Hill, London, W11 2RH
- 44b Pimlico Road, Pimlico, London, SW1W 8LP

The Deli at No.5 www.thedeliatno5.co.uk
- 73 Giffard Way, Long Crendon, Buckinghamshire, HP18 9DN

The East Street Deli www.theeaststreetdeli.co.uk
- 41b East Street, Wimborne, Dorset, BH21 1DX

The Fine Cheese Company www.finecheeseshops.co.uk
- 29 - 31 Walcot Street, Bath, BA1 5BN

Forest Deli www.forest-deli.co.uk
- 4 Market Place, Coleford, Gloucestershire

Friday Street Farm Shop www.fridaystfarm.co.uk
- Friday Street Farm, Farnham, Suffolk, IP17 1JX

George & Joseph www.georgeandjoseph.co.uk
- 140 Harrogate Road, Chapel Allerton, Leeds, LS7 4NZ

George Mewes www.georgemewescheese.co.uk
- 106 Byres Road, Glasgow, G12 8TB
- 3 Dean Park Street, Stockbridge, Edinburgh, EH4 1JN

Godalming Food Company www.godalmingfood.co.uk
- 1 Angel Court, Godalming, Surrey, GU7 1AQ

Godfrey C. Williams www.godfreycwilliams.co.uk
- 9/11 The Square, Sandbach, Cheshire, CW11 1AP

Goo Cheese www.goo-cheese.co.uk
▭ 2 Carlton House, Hebden Bridge, West Yorkshire, HX7 8ES

Grate Newcastle www.gratenewcastle.co.uk
▭ 252 Jesmond Road, Jesmond, Newcastle upon Tyne, NE2 1LD

Green and Lovely www.greenandlovely.co.uk
▭ 8 Bridge Road, East Molesey, Surrey, KT8 9HA

Hamish Johnston www.hamishjohnston.com
▭ 48 Northcote Road, Battersea, London, SW11 1PA

Hampshire Deli www.hampshire-deli.co.uk
▭ Wolverton Park, Ramsdell Road, Wolverton, RG26 5PU

Heritage Cheese www.heritagecheese.uk
▭ 1b Calton Avenue, Dulwich, London, SE21 7DE

I.J. Mellis www.mellischeese.net
▭ 30a Victoria Street, Edinburgh, EH1 2JW
▭ 330 Morningside Road, Edinburgh, EH10 4QJ
▭ 6 Bakers Place, Stockbridge, Edinburgh, EH3 6SY
▭ 492 Great Western Road, Glasgow, G12 8EW
▭ 149 South Street, St Andrews, KY16 9UN

Jericho Cheese Company www.jerichocheese.co.uk
▭ 25 Little Clarendon Street, Oxford, Oxfordshire, OX1 2HU
▭ 7 St Michael's Mansions, Ship Street, Oxford, Oxfordshire, OX1 3DE

Knowles Green www.knowlesgreen.uk
▭ 114 Wellington Road, Bollington, Cheshire, SK10 5HT

La Fromagerie www.lafromagerie.co.uk
▭ 2-6 Moxon Street, Marylebone, London, W1U 4EW
▭ 30 Highbury Park, London, N5 2AA
▭ 52 Lamb's Conduit Street, London, Wax Coated1N 3LL

Lewis & Cooper   www.lewisandcooper.co.uk
92 High Street, Northallerton, North Yorkshire, DL7 8PT

The Little Cheesemonger   www.thelittlecheesemonger.co.uk
87 High Street, Prestatyn, Denbighshire, LL19 9AP

Liverpool Cheese Company   www.liverpoolcheesecompany.com
29a Woolton Street, Liverpool, Merseyside, L25 5NH

London Cheesemongers   www.londoncheesemongersco.uk
251 Pavilion Road, Belgravia, London, SW1 0BP

Love Cheese   www.lovecheese.co.uk
16 Gillygate, York, North Yorkshire, YO31 7EQ

MacFarlane's Delicatessen   www.macfarlanesdeli.co.uk
48 Abbeville Road, Clapham, London, SW4 9NF

Macknade   www.macknade.com
Selling Road, Faversham, Kent, ME13 8XF

Madame Fromage   www.madamefromage.co.uk
16 Neville Street, Abergavenny, Monmouthshire, NP7 5AD

Magdalen Cheese & Provisions   www.magdalencheese.co.uk
71 Magdalen Road, Exeter, Devon, EX2 4TA

Mike's Fancy Cheese   www.mfcheese.com
41 Little Donegall Street, Belfast, BT1 2JD

Mons Cheesemongers   www.mons-cheese.co.uk
153 Lordship Lane, East Dulwich, SE22 8HX

The Mousetrap Cheeseshop www.mousetrapcheese.co.uk
- 6 Church Street, Ludlow, Herefordshire, SY8 1AP
- 3 School Lane, Leominster, Herefordshire, HR6 8AA
- 30 Church Street, Hereford, Herefordshire, HR1 2LR

Neal's Yard Dairy www.nealsyarddairy.co.uk
- 9 Park Street, Borough Market, London, SE1 9AB
- Arch 8, Lucy Way, Bermondsey, London, SE16 3UF
- 17 Shorts Gardens, Seven Dials, London, Wax Coated2H 9AT

Newlyns Farm Shop www.newlyns-farmshop.co.uk
- Lodge Farm North, Warnborough, Hampshire, RG29 1HA

No2 Pound Street www.2poundstreet.com
- No.2 Pound Street, Wendover, HP22 6EJ

The Norfolk Deli www.norfolk-deli.co.uk
- 16 Greevegate, Hunstanton, Norfolk, PE36 6AA

Oxford Cheese Company www.oxfordcheese.co.uk
- The Covered Market, Market Street, Oxford, Oxfordshire, OX1 3DU

Parsnips www.parsnips.shop
- 16 High Street, Teddington, London, TW11 8EW

Paxton & Whitfield www.paxtonandwhitfield.co.uk
- 93 Jermyn Street, London, SW1Y 6JE
- 22 Cale Street, Chelsea, London, SW3 3QU
- 13 Wood Street, Stratford-upon-Avon, Warwickshire, CV37 6JF
- 1 John Street, Bath, Somerset, BA1 2JL

Pick & Cheese www.thecheesebar.com
- Pick & Cheese, Seven Dials Market, Seven Dials, London, WC2H 9LD

Pong Cheese www.pongcheese.co.uk
- Online only

Provender Brown www.provenderbrown.co.uk
- 23 George Street, Perth, PH1 5JY

Rennet and Rind www.rennetandrind.co.uk
- 16 High Street, Stamford, Lincolnshire, PE9 2AL
- 62 - 64 Papworth Business Park, Papworth, Cambridgeshire, CB23 3GY

Rind (Restaurant) www.thecheesebar.com
- The Courtyard Dairy, Austwick, North Yorkshire, LA2 8AS

Rippon Cheese Store www.ripponcheeselondon.com
- 26 Upper Tachbrook Street, Pimlico, London, SW1V 1SW

St Giles Cheese www.facebook.com/stgilescheese
- 77 St Giles Street, Northampton, NN1 1JF

Star Plain www.starplain.com
- 8 Fish Hill, Holt, Norfolk, NR25 6BD

Teddington Cheese www.teddingtoncheese.co.uk
- 42 Station Road, Teddington, London, TW11 9AA
- 74 Hill Rise, Richmond, Surrey, TW10 6UB

Tŷ Caws www.tycaws.com
- 28 Castle Arcade, Cardiff, CF10 1BY

Victoria's Cheese www.victoriascheese.co.uk
- 28a High Street, Ely, Cambridgeshire, CB7 4JU

Welbeck Farm Shop www.welbeckfarmshop.co.uk
- Welbeck Estate, Worksop, Nottinghamshire, S80 3LW

The Welsh Cheese Company www.welshcheesecompany.co.uk
13 Rombourne Business Centre, Taff's Well, Mid Glamorgan, CF15 7QR

If you know of a cheesemonger or cheese restaurant that you feel should be included in future books and future editions of this book, please drop me an e-mail at steve@steveparkercheeseandwine.com

Index of Cheeses

MILK : C = Cow   G = Goat   S = Sheep   B = Buffalo
TREATMENT : U = Unpasteurised   P = Pasteurised   T = Thermised
UP = Unpasteurised or Pasteurised
RENNET : A = Animal (Traditional)   V = Vegetarian   L = Lactic
AV = Both Animal and Vegetarian
ORGANIC : O = Organic

Name of Cheese	Dairy	Milk				Page
A						
Abaty Glas	Caws Pen Helyg	C	U	V	O	61
Ailsa Craig	Dunlop Dairy	G	P	V		107
Airedale	Eldwick Creamery	C	P	V		96
Ancient Ashmore	Cheesemakers of Canterbury	C	U	V		140
Anster	St Andrews Cheese Co.	C	U	A		21
Appleby's Cheshire	Appleby's	C	U	A		136
Ashcombe	King Stone Dairy	C	P	A	O	38
Ashdown Forester	High Weald Dairy	C	P	V	O	44
Ashmore Farmhouse	Cheesemakers of Canterbury	C	U	V		47
Auld Lochnagar	Cambus O'May Cheese Co.	C	U	A		98
Austen	Book & Bucket Cheese Co.	S	P	V		77
Ayrshire Dunlop	Dunlop Dairy	C	P	V		72
B						
Balcombe Breeze	Balcombe Dairy	C	P	V		31
Barber's 1833 Vintage Reserve	Barber's Farmhouse Cheese	C	P	V	O	134
Barkham Blue	Village Maid Cheese	C	P	V		115
Baron Bigod	Fen Farm Dairy	C	P	A		67
Batch Farm Cheddar	Batch Farm Cheesemakers	C	P	AV		36
Batch Farm Curds	Batch Farm Cheesemakers	C	U	V		26
Bath Soft	Bath Soft Cheese Co.	C	P	A	O	67
Beacon Fell	Dewlay Cheesemakers	C	P	V		113
Beauvale	Cropwell Bishop Creamery	C	P	A		79

Belton Farm Cheshire	Belton Farm	C	P	V		136
Bermondsey Frier	Kappacasein	C	U	A	O	77
Bermondsey Hard Pressed	Kappacasein	C	U	A	O	98
Bevistan Tomme	Bevistan Dairy	S	P	V		91
Biggar Blue	Errington Cheese	G	U	V		105
Birdoswald	Slack House Farm	C	P	V	O	21
Bix	Nettlebed Creamery	C	P	A	O	67
Black Bomber	Snowdonia Cheese Co.	C	P	V		61
Bledington Blue	Daylesford Organics	C	P	V	O	49
Blue Bay	Country Cheeses	C	P	V		138
Blue Clouds	Balcombe Dairy	C	P	V		79
Blue Millie	Cheese on the Wey	C	T	V		138
Blue Murder	Highland Fine Cheeses	C	P	V		49
Blue Wenalt	Brooke's Wye Valley Dairy	C	P	V		61
Bonnington Linn	Errington Cheese	G	U	A		121
Briddlesford Cheddar	Briddlesford Farm Dairy	C	P	V		23
Brighton Blue	High Weald Dairy	C	P	V		54
Brue Valley Fior di Latte	Brue Valley	C	P	V		49
Bruton Beauty	Godminster Cheese	C	P	V	O	82
Buffalicious Mozzarella	West Country Water Buffalo	B	U	V		51
Buffalo Blue	Shepherds Purse Cheeses	B	P	V		124
Burt's Blue	Burt's Cheese	C	P	V		79

C

Caerfai Caerffili	Caerfai Farm	C	U	V	O	61
Calveley Mill Mozzarella	Calveley Mill	C	P	V		51
Cathedral City Vintage	Davidstow Creamery	C	P	V		134
Caws Chwaral	Cosyn Cymru	S	U	A		61
Caws Dyfi	Aberdyfi Cheese Co.	S	P	A		61
Charlton	Goodwood Home Farm	C	P	V	O	44
Cheddar Gorge Cheddar	Cheddar Gorge Cheese Co.	C	U	V		36
Chiltern Cloud	Marlow Cheese Co	S	P	V	O	52
Cobblers Nibble	Hamm Tun Fine Foods	C	U	V		103
Colliers Powerful Cheddar	Fayrefield Foods	C	P	V		134

Colston Bassett Stilton	Colston Bassett Dairy	C	P	AV		75
Cornish Blue	Cornish Cheese Co.	C	P	V		115
Cornish Camembert	Cornish Cheese Co.	C	P	V		70
Cornish Kern	Lynher Dairies	C	P	A		140
Cornish Nanny	Cornish Cheese Co.	G	P	V		105
Corra Linn	Errington Cheese	S	U	A		119
Cote Hill Red	Cote Hill Farm	C	U	V		100
Cropwell Bishop Stilton	Cropwell Bishop Creamery	C	P	AV		75
Crump's Double Gloucester	Jonathan Crump's	C	U	V		128
Crump's Single Gloucester	Jonathan Crump's	C	U	V		130
Cumberland Farmhouse	Thornby Moor Dairy	C	U	A		41
Curthwaite	Thornby Moor Dairy	G	U	V		107

D

Dale End Cheddar	Botton Creamery	C	U	V	O	28
Daylesford Double Gloucester	Daylesford Organics	C	P	A	O	128
Daylesford Single Gloucester	Daylesford Organics	C	P	A	O	130
Demeter	Wildcroft Dairy	G	U	A		77
Devon Blue	Ticklemore Cheese Dairy	C	P	V		79
Devonshire Red	Quicke's Traditional	C	P	V		56
Dirty Vicar	Norbury Park Farm Cheese	C	U	V		85
Doris	Teesdale Cheesemakers	C	P	V		85
Dorset Blue Vinny	Woodbridge Farm	C	P	V		54
Double Devonshire	Quicke's Traditional	C	P	V		82
Dovedale Blue	Staffordshire Cheese Co.	C	P	V		124
Duddleswell	High Weald Dairy	S	P	V		119

E

East Lee	Pextenement Cheese Co.	C	P	V	O	136
Eden Chieftain	Appleby Creamery	C	P	V		41

F

Fallen Monk	Lacey's Cheese	S	U	V	96
Fat Cow	Highland Fine Cheeses	C	P	V	31

Federia	Larkton Hall Cheese	C	U	A		87
Fellstone	Whin Yeats Dairy	C	U	A		96
Fetish	White Lake Cheese	S	T	V		64
Ffetys	Y Cwt Caws	G	P	V		64
Fosse Way Fleece	Somerset Cheese Co.	S	P	V		49

G

Gert Lush	Feltham's Farm Cheeses	C	P	V	O	70
Godsell's Single Gloucester	Godsell's Cheese	C	P	V		130
Golden Cenarth	Caws Cenarth	C	P	V	O	85
Green's Twanger	Greens of Glastonbury	C	P	V		126
Greenfields Lancashire	Greenfields Dairy Products	C	P	V		113
Greystones Single Gloucester	Simon Weaver Organic	C	P	V	O	130
Guernsleigh Original	Guernsleigh Cheese	C	P	V		132

H

Hafod	Holden Farm Dairy	C	UP	A	O	28
Harbourne Blue	Ticklemore Cheese Dairy	G	P	V		105
Hardy's	Book & Bucket Cheese Co.	S	P	V		119
Harefield	Smart's Traditional	C	U	V		52
Hartington Stilton	Hartington Creamery	C	P	V		75
Haytor	Curworthy Cheese	C	P	V		33
High Weald Ricotta	High Weald Dairy	S	P	V	O	51
Highmoor	Nettlebed Creamery	C	P	A	O	85
Holbrook	St James Cheese	G	U	A		31
Hollywell	Monmouth Shepherd	S	P	V		61

I

Idle Hour	Alsop & Walker	C	P	V		44
Isle of Mull Cheddar	Isle of Mull Cheese	C	U	A		28

K

Kappacasein Ricotta	Kappacasein	C	U	A	O	51
Kearney Blue	Farmview Dairies	C	P	A		93

Kedar Ricotta	The Kedar Cheese Co.	C	P	V		51
Keen's Cheddar	Keen's	C	U	A		72
Kelly's Canterbury Goat	Cheesemakers of Canterbury	G	U	V		121
Kingcott Blue	Kingcott Dairy	C	U	V		115
Kit Calvert Wensleydale	Wensleydale Creamery	C	P	V		111
Knuckleduster	Lincolnshire Poacher Cheese	C	U	A		140

L

La Latteria Fior di latte	La Latteria	C	P	A		49
Lanark Blue	Errington Cheese	S	U	V		54
Leeds Blue	Yorkshire Pecorino	S	P	A		115
Leno	Hand Stretched Cheese	C	P	V	O	49
Leonard Stanley	Godsell's Cheese	C	P	V		132
Lincolnshire Poacher	Lincolnshire Poacher Cheese	C	U	A		100
Lincolnshire Red	Lincolnshire Poacher Cheese	C	U	V		56
Lion Hotel 1868 Cheddar	Blaenafon Cheddar Co.	C	P	V		23
Little Hereford	Monkland Cheese Dairy	C	U	V		98
Llain	Caws Cenarth	C	P	V	O	87
London Raclette	Kappacasein	C	U	A	O	89
Long Clawson Stilton	Long Clawson Dairy	C	P	V		75
Long Lane Ricotta	Long Lane Dairy	S	P	V		51
Lord of the Hundreds	Traditional Cheese Dairy	S	U	V		98
Lye Cross Mature Cheddar	Lye Cross Farm	C	P	V		126

M

Martell's Double Gloucester	Charles Martell & Son	C	UP	V		128
Mayfield	Alsop & Walker	C	P	V		89
Medita	High Weald Dairy	S	P	V		64
Meeny Hill Blue	Dart Mountain Cheese	G	P	V		93
Minger	Highland Fine Cheeses	C	P	V		85
Mon Las	Caws Rhyd Y Delyn	C	P	V		61
Montgomery's Cheddar	Montgomery's Cheeses	C	U	A		36
Moorland Tomme	Botton Creamery	C	U	V	O	91
Morn Dew	White Lake Cheese	C	P	V		72

Mount's Bay Mozzarella	The Buffalo Dairy	B	P	V		51
Mrs Bell's Salad Cheese	Shepherds Purse Cheeses	S	P	V		64
Mrs Bourne's Cheshire	Mrs Bourne's Cheese	C	P	V		136
Mrs Kirkham's Curds	Mrs Kirkham's Lancashire	C	U	A		26
Mrs Kirkham's Lancashire	Mrs Kirkham's Lancashire	C	U	A		113

N

Nanny Blue	Teesdale Cheesemakers	G	P	V		105
Norbury Blue	Norbury Park Farm Cheese	C	U	V		138
Norfolk Dapple Vintage	Ferndale Norfolk Cheeses	C	U	V		21
Northamptonshire Blue	Hamm Tun Fine Foods	C	U	V		54

O

Ogleshield	Montgomery's Cheeses	C	U	A		89
Old Winchester	Lyburn farmhouse Cheese	C	P	V		140
Olde Sussex	Traditional Cheese Dairy	C	U	V		44
Olwyn Fawr	Cosyn Cymru	S	U	A		61
Ottinge Bramshill	Ottinge Court Dairy	C	U	A		47

P

Perl Las	Caws Cenarth	C	P	V	O	61
Perroche	Neal's Yard Creamery	G	P	V		107
Pevensey Blue	Pevensey Cheese Co.	C	P	A		138
Phipps Firkin	Northampton Cheese Co.	C	P	V	O	103
Pitchfork Cheddar	Trethowan Brothers	C	U	A	O	38
Plaw Hatch Cheddar	Plaw Hatch Farm	C	U	V	O	23

Q

Quicke's Cheddar	Quicke's Traditional	C	P	AV		126
Quicke's Goat	Quicke's Traditional	G	P	V		121

R

Rachael Reserva	White Lake Cheese	G	T	V		89
Rachel	White Lake Cheese	G	T	V		121

Rainton Tomme	The Ethical Dairy	C	U	V	O	91
Ramps Hill	Brinkworth Dairy	C	P	V		33
Ramsey	Cheesemakers of Canterbury	S	U	V		49
Red Fox	Belton Farm	C	P	V		56
Redesdale	Northumberland Cheese Co.	S	P	V		49
Regatta	Marlow Cheese Co	C	P	V		33
Rollright	King Stone Dairy	C	P	A	O	59
Rosary	Rosary Goat's Cheese	G	P	V		107

S

Scottish Buffalo Mozzarella	The Buffalo Farm	B	P	V		51
Seriously Strong Vintage	Caledonian Creamery	C	P	V		134
Shoetown Blue	Hamm Tun Fine Foods	C	U	V		124
Six Spires	Somerset Cheese Co.	C	U	V		72
Sizzler	Plaw Hatch Farm	C	U	V	O	77
Smart's Double Gloucester	Smart's Traditional	C	U	V		128
Somerset Goat Halloumi	White Lake Cheese	G	T	V		77
Sparkenhoe Red Leicester	Leicestershire Handmade	C	U	A		56
Spenwood	Village Maid Cheese	S	T	V		119
Sperrin Blue	Dart Mountain Cheese	C	P	V		93
St Benedict	Lacey's Cheese	S	U	V		49
St Sunday	St James Cheese	C	P	V		59
Stichelton	Stichelton Dairy	C	U	A		38
Stinking Bishop	Charles Martell & Son	C	P	V		59
Stonebeck	Stonebeck Cheese	C	U	A		111
Stow Blue	Cotswold Cheese Co	C	P	V		124
Summerfield Alpine	Botton Creamery	C	U	V	O	33
Sunday Best	Butlers Farmhouse Cheeses	C	P	V		113
Sussex Camembert	Alsop & Walker	C	P	V		70
Sussex Charmer	Bookham Harrison	C	P	V		82
Swaledale	Swaledale Cheese Co.	C	P	V		111

T

Tam's Tipple	Hinxden Farm Dairy	C	U	V	47

Teesdale Blue	Teesdale Cheesemakers	C	P	V		49
Teifi Caerphilly	Caws Teifi	C	U	A	O	61
The English Pecorino	White Lake Cheese	S	T	V		52
Thelma's Traditional Caerphilly	Caws Cenarth	C	P	V	O	61
Times Past Traditional Cheddar	Times Past Cheese Dairy	C	P	V		126
Tirkeeran	Dart Mountain Cheese	C	P	A		52
Tommie	Cheese on the Wey	C	T	V		91
Tongue Taster	Northampton Cheese Co.	C	P	V	O	103
Trusmadoor	Torpenhow Farmhouse Dairy	C	P	V	O	41
Tunworth	Hampshire Cheeses	C	P	A		70

V

Valley Drover	Hancocks Meadow Farm	S	U	A		87
Velocheese	Velocheese	C	P	A	O	49
Volesdale	Coachyard Creamery	C	U	V		82

W

Wandering Ewe	Wandering Ewe Dairy	S	U	A		31
Wash Stone	Whin Yeats Dairy	C	U	A		41
Waterloo	Village Maid Cheese	C	T	V		67
Weardale	Weardale Cheese	C	P	V		132
Wells Alpine	Mrs Temple's Cheese	C	P	V		87
Westcombe Cheddar	Westcombe Dairy	C	U	A		28
Westcombe Curds	Westcombe Dairy	C	U	A		26
Weywood	Cheese on the Wey	C	T	V		85
Wiggold Cheddar	Abbey Home Farm	C	P	V	O	23
Wighton	Mrs Temple's Cheese	C	P	V		77
Wiltshire Loaf	Brinkworth Dairy	C	P	V		21
Winslade	Hampshire Cheeses	C	P	A		59
Winterdale Shaw	Winterdale Cheesemakers	C	U	A		47
Wookey Hole Cheddar	Ford Farm Cheesemakers	C	P	V		36
Wyfe of Bath	Bath Soft Cheese Co	C	P	V	O	132

Y

Yester Farm Fior di Latte	Yester Farm Dairies	C	P	V	26
Yoredale	Curlew Dairy	C	U	AV	111
Yorkshire Blue	Shepherds Purse Cheeses	C	P	V	49
Yorkshire Pecorino	Yorkshire Pecorino	S	P	A	96
Yorkshire Squeaky Cheese	Yorkshire Dama Cheese	C	P	V	77
Young Buck	Mike's Fancy Cheese Co.	C	U	A	93

General Index

A

Almonds	45
Ancre Hill Chardonnay (Wine)	62
Apple	22, 27, 81
Apple Juice	36, 80, 126
Apple Sauce	112
Ark Ripasso Noir (Wine)	26
Asparagus	125

B

Babu's Vineyard Late Harvest Solaris (Wine)	80
Bacon - Streaky	20, 29, 57, 74, 86, 97
Baking Powder	71, 101, 122, 133
Balfour Springfield Chardonnay (Wine)	67
Barnsole Pinot Précoce (Wine)	26
Basil - Dried	63, 133
Becket's Honey Ale (Beer)	103
Beef Mince	37
Beef Stock	24
Beer	32, 36, 101
Bicarbonate of Soda	122
Biddenden Schönburger (Wine)	115
Black Olives	63, 76
Blackboys Vineyard Tickerage Chardonnay (Wine)	44
Bluebell Vineyard Ashdown Chasselas (Wine)	44
Branston Pickle	27
Bread - Bloomer	27
Bread - Granary	20, 27
Bread - Sliced	22, 35
Breadcrumbs - Fresh	46, 48, 53, 55, 63, 99, 106
Broccoli	106
Brown Rice	45
Brussels Sprouts	29, 99
Burn Valley Rondo (Wine)	26

Burn Valley Solar (Wine)	80
Burrow Hill Sparkling (Cider)	36
Butter	20, 22, 24, 29, 43, 45, 48, 55, 57, 60, 66, 69, 71, 79, 84, 86, 88, 90, 94, 99, 101, 104, 106, 110, 122, 125, 127, 131, 133, 135
Butter Beans	97

C

Cabbage	29, 81
Capers	63
Carrot	45, 81, 106, 125
Cashew Nuts	45
Cauliflower	106, 125
Celery	81, 125
Celery Salt	50
Chapel Down Kits Coty Chardonnay (Wine)	67
Chestnut Mushroom	21, 31, 45, 66, 104
Chick Peas	76
Chicken Breast	66
Chicken Stock	43, 60, 94
Chocolate (Dark) Hobnob	114
Cider	22, 34, 35, 125
Cider Vinegar	74, 81
Cobnuts	45
Cornflour	32
Courgette	50, 106
Cranberries - Dried	53
Cream - Soured	57
Cream Cheese	79, 94
Crème Fraiche	20, 27, 48, 66, 69, 81, 90, 99
Crystallised Ginger	110

Cucumber	76
Cumberland Sausage	40
Cumin	97

D

Dark Chocolate Hobnob	114
Demerara Sugar	110
Denbies Noble Harvest (Wine)	80
Dried Basil	63, 133
Dried Oregano	76
Dried Parsley	133
Dried Sage	22, 35, 40, 46, 53, 55, 71, 88, 94, 133, 135
Dried Thyme	66, 69, 133
Dunesforde Pinot Gris (Wine)	96

E

Egg	20, 37, 40, 46, 53, 63, 71, 87, 94, 101, 106, 112, 122, 127, 131, 135
Eglantine North Star (Wine)	115
English Mustard	22, 35
Exton Park RB|45 Blanc de Blancs (Wine)	67

F

Fennel Seeds	50
Flour - Plain	24, 35, 40, 63, 71, 86, 92, 94, 110, 112, 122, 127, 129, 131, 133
Flour - Self Raising	101
Flour - Wholemeal	122
Fresh Breadcrumbs	46, 48, 53, 55, 63, 99, 106
Fresh Mint	76
Fruit Cake	112

G

Garlic	24, 32, 45, 57, 69, 90, 97, 104, 125
Garlic Granules / Powder	133
Gherkin	57
Ginger - Crystallised	110
Gnocchi	48
Gold Star (Beer)	103
Green Olives	78
Green Pepper	125

H

Ham	27
Harrow Hope Blanc de Blancs (Wine)	67
Hattingley Valley Entice (Wine)	115
Hazelnuts	45
Hiver Amber (Beer)	34
Hobnob - Dark Chocolate	114
Honey	74, 80, 81, 110, 118, 121, 122, 139
Horseradish	101
Hundred Hills Blanc de Blancs (Wine)	67

I

Innes & Gunn Caribbean Rum Cask (Beer)	34

J

Jammie Dodgers	115

K

Kale	29

L

Laurel Vines Solaris (Wine)	96

Leek	60
Lemon Juice	32, 71
Lemon - Preserved	63
Lettuce - Little Gem	74
Lettuce - Romaine	76
Little Gem Lettuce	74
Little Pomona Orchard Yarlington Mill (Cider)	36
Llanerch Cariad Poplar White (Wine)	62

M

Mangetout	50
Mango	120
Marmalade	120
Midsummer Meadow (Beer)	103
Milk	40, 71, 94, 122
Mint - Fresh	76
Montgomery Seyval Solaris (Wine)	62
Mushroom - Chestnut	21, 31, 45, 66, 104
Mustard - English	22, 35, 103
Mustard - Wholegrain	74, 81

N

Nectarine	121
New Hall Purlai Gold (Wine)	80
Nutbourne Hedgerow (Wine)	44
Nutmeg	99
Nuts - Mixed	45

O

Oastbrook Chardonnay (Wine)	67
Oil - Rapeseed	24, 29, 37, 43, 50, 53, 63, 71, 74, 76, 81, 84, 86, 92, 94, 97, 99, 101, 104, 133
Olives - Black	63, 76

Olives - Green	78
Onion	22, 40, 43, 45, 55, 57, 63, 76, 81, 86, 94, 104, 135
Onion - Pickled	27
Onion - Spring	28, 29, 43, 50, 92, 106
Oregano - Dried	76
Oxney Chardonnay	67

P

Paprika	133
Paprika - Smoked	
Parsley - Dried	133
Pastry - Puff	37, 57, 112
Pear	23, 28, 74, 111, 118, 121
Pearl Barley	60
Pepper - Green / Red	125
Pesto	50
Pickle - Branston	27
Pickled Onion	27
Pilton Star Ship (Cider)	36
Pistachio Nut Kernels	76
Plain Flour	24, 35, 40, 63, 71, 86, 92, 94, 110, 112, 122, 127, 129, 131, 133
Plain Yogurt	122
Porridge Oats	110, 135
Potatoes	24, 29, 43, 57, 69, 84, 86, 88, 90, 92
Pastry - Puff	37, 57
Pizza Base	50
Preserved Lemon	63
Puff Pastry	37, 57, 112
Pumpkin Seeds	78

R

Rapeseed Oil	24, 29, 37, 43, 50, 53, 63, 71, 74, 76, 81, 84, 86, 92, 94, 97, 99, 101, 104, 133
Red Cabbage	81
Red Pepper	125
Rhubarb	110
Rice - Brown	45
Ridgeview Blanc de Blancs (Wine)	67
Rocket	74
Romaine Lettuce	76
Ryedale Yorkshire's Lass (Wine)	96

S

Sage - Dried	22, 35, 40, 46, 53, 55, 71, 88, 94, 133, 135
Sausages	40, 53
Self Raising Flour	101
Sesame Seeds	78
Shallot	20, 24, 37, 66, 69, 88, 97
Smoked Paprika	97
Solar Star (Beer)	103
Soured Cream	57
Spinach	48
Spring Onion	28, 29, 43, 50, 92, 106
St Peter's Golden Ale (Beer)	34
Stock - Beef	24
Stock - Chicken	43, 60, 94
Stock - Vegetable	62
Stopham Estate Pinot Blanc (Wine)	44
Sugar - Demerara	110
Sundried Tomatoes	63
Sunflower Seeds	78

T

Tenderstem Broccoli	50
Thyme - Dried	66, 69, 133
Toast	125
Tomato	76
Tomato - Sundried	63
Tomato - Tinned Chopped	97
Tomato Purée	45, 97
Trevibban Mill Black Ram Red (Wine)	26

V

Vegemite	132
Vegetable Stock	62
Vinegar - Cider	74, 81

W

Walnuts	45, 48, 53, 74, 140
Watercress	74
White Cabbage	81
White Castle Gwin Gwyn (Wine)	62
Wholegrain Mustard	74, 81
Wholemeal Flour	122
Wilding Ditcheat Hill (Cider)	36
Windsor & Eton Knight of the Garter (Beer)	34
Wine	24, 43, 60, 66, 79, 94, 114
Worcestershire Sauce	24, 35

Y

Yeast Extract	131
Yogurt - Plain	122
Yorkshire Heart Winemaker's Choice (Wine)	96

www.steveparkercheeseandwine.com

steve@steveparkercheeseandwine.com

Twitter : @stevecheesewine

Instagram : stevecheesewine

Facebook : Steve Parker Cheese and Wine

Other Books from Steve Parker

- 📖 British Cheese on Toast
- 📖 British Cheese Spotting

Future Books from Steve Parker

- 📖 British Wine Spotting
- 📖 British Cheese and Wine Pairing
- 📖 Lost Cheeses of Britain
- 📖 Cheddar and Chardonnay (A Novel)

Printed in Dunstable, United Kingdom

65363009R00100